**PRINT CASEBOOKS 6/1984-85 EDITION
THE BEST IN ANNUAL REPORTS**

1984/85 Edition

PRINT CASEBOOKS 6
The Best in
ANNUAL REPORTS

Written by
Rose M. DeNeve

Published by
**RC Publications, Inc.
Bethesda, MD**

First published 1984 in the
United States of America
by RC Publications, Inc.
6400 Goldsboro Road
Bethesda, MD 20817

All rights reserved. No part of this publication may be reproduced or used in any form or by any means—graphic, electronic, or mechanical, including photocopying, recording, taping, or information storage and retrieval systems—without written permission of the publisher.

Manufactured in Hong Kong
First Printing 1984

PRINT CASEBOOKS 6/1984-85 EDITION/THE BEST IN ANNUAL REPORTS
Library of Congress Catalog Card Number 75-649581
ISBN 0-915734-42-7

PRINT CASEBOOKS 6/1984-85 EDITION
Complete 6-Volume Set
ISBN 0-915734-40-0

RC PUBLICATIONS
President and Publisher: Howard Cadel
Vice President and Editor: Martin Fox
Art Director/Designer: Andrew P. Kner
Managing Editor: Teresa Reese
Associate Art Director: Carol Stevens Kner
Assistant Editor: Tom Goss
Graphic Production: Rea Ackerman
Production Assistant: Susan Norr

Introduction

Over the years, an annual or bi-annual survey of the best in graphic design, such as the Print Casebooks, creates a rare vantage point. First, it allows an overview of what's happening in the world of design as a whole—or within the sphere of a particular volume—at any given time. But—and more importantly—the Casebooks as a series provide a larger context in which to view these designs: Different solutions to similar problems can be compared and contrasted through time; trends can be spotted and documented as they develop; insights can be gained into movements reaching far beyond the borders of graphic design.

This last point is especially true of annual report design. An area of specialization comprising a large share of today's design market, it sits atop the nerve center of our economy itself. Anyone with a modicum of experience in looking at these glossy little financial documents quickly reads beyond the dazzle to the bottom line. And yet, a well-designed annual report can impart a feeling of professionalism and competence about a particular company, even if that bottom line isn't so good.

In looking back over the nearly ten years of annual reports collected into Casebooks, we see an interesting picture emerge. What it reveals doesn't have so much to do with the *design* of annual reports as with the uses to which they have been put. Indeed, as a form, the annual report has changed little in those years, no doubt because the basic message of the non-regulated areas of the report is still the same: The corporation is strong, its employees responsible, its products reliable, its management savvy. Moreover, there is something to be said for a form that can meet so well the needs of boom years as well as bad.

But where once the annual report sought primarily to position a corporation as imposing and well-organized in general terms, today's annual reports are becoming more specific. And the change, it appears, has to do with some shifts in corporate thinking about annual reports—shifts that have come in response to social and economic pressures.

In the past few years, increasing numbers of companies have been using the annual report as a platform to make a position statement. At first, the topic was likely to be political—comments on government regulation of industry, perhaps, or corporate responsibility and the environment. While such editorializing was confined to a specific area of the report, it often served to soften the image of the corporation as a faceless and all-powerful giant. The giant may be powerful, these personal-sounding documents seemed to say, but it's also human.

More recently, this vertical compartmentalization has been turned to more intimate needs, and in some cases a special essay section becomes the major focus of the report. Production values once poured into the operations section are now being diverted into a photo essay that stresses international markets, or accounts for the millions of dollars a company has spent on product research and development. In books like these, the operations review is apt to be reduced to a few spot-illustrated pages, or folded entirely into the financial report. In other books—those following a more conventional format—the essay may be something of a "white paper" that appears, simple and unadorned, at the front of the operations review.

Clearly, corporations have felt the need, in these economically troubled times, to address specific problems within their industries, or to focus on their particular strengths. As new and more creative instruments have opened up financial investing to more and more people, these people have become increasingly sophisticated about the financial marketplace; average, ordinary citizens have begun to make inroads into what was once the analyst's domain.

And so the annual report in turn has become the place for a broadly issued but tightly focussed declaration of strategy. A company may be having a hard time—but so are we all. And when the bottom line fails to draw attention, the next best thing is to tell people what's being done about it—and why.

Beyond content and form, the effects of the recent recession can be seen in other aspects of the annual report. As might be expected, most reports are conservatively styled, with less ornamentation than in more prosperous times, and what we do see by way of embellishment is sure to be useful as well.

In terms of production, most designers still selected premium sheets for four- to six-color reproduction, but, as budgets were reduced or frozen, some were doing smaller books. There was a noticeable increase in the number of two-color books in this Casebook competition—fully a third of the winners were printed in black-and-white—perhaps with a duotone for halftones and a third color for highlights.

There was also a larger number of double saddle-stitched books entered this year. Once, designers who wanted to combine papers or cluster production effects had to use perfect binding—and that calls for a sizable book. But now, thanks to improvements in saddle-stitching, smaller reports can utilize two papers and split runs, too, and they end up looking better for less.

Perhaps because of those tightened purse strings, only two of the reports in this Casebook—those for Eli Lilly and Knudsen—were unanimously elected to appear. Most of the reports here received only the minimum three out of five votes necessary to be declared a winner, a fact suggesting that there was little in the way of truly innovative design in the present crop of reports. Many competently designed and beautifully executed reports were rejected simply because they had nothing new to offer.

After a first round of judging over 700 reports, only a handful more than the required 30 remained for final selection in the second round—as compared with other, presumably more dynamic years, where sometimes more than twice that number survived round one. Other interesting statistics: Only 12 of the winners are in an 8½" by 11" format, and more than 50 per cent utilize both text and coated papers.

And what were the jurors looking for? After they had discussed the relative importance of typographic handling, graphic styling, printing values, and overall execution, juror Bennett Robinson seemed to sum up all of the jurors' criteria: "The bottom line question is, does it tell you anything? In a successful report, each page has to have something to say."—*Rose DeNeve*

Casebook Jurors

Al Gluth

After graduating from Art Center College of Design in Los Angeles, Al Gluth worked as senior art director for several Houston firms before joining John Weaver in the formation of Gluth, Weaver, Inc., in 1977. The Houston firm has established itself as one of the leading design firms in the field of corporate communication, receiving widespread recognition for its design and production of annual reports. Their work has appeared in various shows and publications, including the *Print Casebooks*, the Mead Library of Ideas and Communication Arts.

Peter Harrison

Peter Harrison was born in London in 1932. After graduating from the London School of Printing, he emigrated to the U.S., training further at Pratt Institute. He worked first with a number of New York advertising agencies, then became involved in projects combining graphics with three-dimensional design. He was responsible for several major exhibitions in Europe and the U.S. and, in 1968, he redesigned the interior and exterior of an ocean liner. He ran his own freelance practice, Harrison Associates, from 1971 until he joined Pentagram in New York in 1979. Harrison has designed annual reports for such companies as American Express, American Standard, Peat Marwick, SCM and Warner Communications. He has received numerous awards.

Michael A. Schacht

Michael A. Schacht has been either selling printing, promoting paper or designing graphics for the past 23 years in New York City. Currently, he is a vice president at Sanders Printing Corp. Active with the recently formed AIGA/NY, Schacht enjoys photography and painting in his spare time.

Carl Seltzer

A full scholarship was Carl Seltzer's reward for distinguishing himself early in his academic years at Art Center College of Design in Los Angeles. After graduating in 1960, he spent his apprentice years in New York City with two well-known packaging and industrial design firms—Donald Deskey, Inc., and Robert Zeidman & Associates. Seltzer was drawn back to Los Angeles as a freelance designer before accepting a permanent position with one of his regular clients, Advertising Designers, Inc. There, he became a vice president and for 13 years produced work for a wide variety of clients. In 1977 he joined Cross Associates. Seltzer has won awards from many graphic design organizations and publications.

Bennett Robinson

A graduate of Syracuse University, Bennett Robinson is chairman and co-founder of Corporate Graphics, Inc., the New York design firm producing annual reports, facilities brochures, corporate identity programs, and other corporate communications. His work has received numerous awards from leading professional organizations. An instructor of design at Pratt Institute for six years, Robinson is currently teaching at New York University.

Casebook Writer

Rose DeNeve

After graduating in design from the State University of New York at Binghamton, Rose DeNeve was for many years on the staff of PRINT. In 1980 she left her managing editor position to freelance as a graphic design consultant to non-profit organizations and as a writer for corporations and for design publications. She recently was named editor of the Journal of the American Institute of Graphic Arts. This is her fourth *Annual Reports Casebook*.

Index

Companies

Amerada Hess 74
Automatic Data Processing, Inc. 22
Champion International 19
Compos Industries, Inc. 30
Convergent Technologies, Inc. 91
Digicon, Inc. 36
Drexel Burnham Lambert 33
Heinz, H.J., Co. 62
Hospital Corporation of America 47
Irving Bank Corp. 10
Knudsen Corp. 59
Lilly, Eli, & Co. 85
Lockheed Corp. 66
Lomas & Nettleton Financial Corp. 68
Lomas & Nettleton Mortgage Investors 42
Management Assistance, Inc. 13
Marline Oil Corp. 94
Northrop Corp. 16
Orthopaedic Hospital 24
Peat Marwick International 82
Pennsylvania Hospital 71
Potlatch Corp. 39
Save The Children 50
SCM Corp. 88
Thermo Electron Corp. 53
Times Mirror Co. 76
Warner Communications, Inc. 56

Design Firms / Designers / Art Directors

Bender, Lawrence 91
Berté, Jim 76
Besser, Rik 59
Boswell, Don 36
Brandon, Linda 91
Burstein, Naomi 13
Corporate Graphics 13, 22, 47, 62, 74, 85
Cross, James 16, 66
Cross Associates 16, 66
Forbes, Colin 33
Gluth, Al 36, 94
Gluth, Weaver 36, 94
Goerke, Henry 50
Harrison, Peter 56, 82
Hatch, James 22
Heiney, John, & Associates 10
Hess, Richard 19
Hess, Richard, Inc. 19
Hinrichs, Kit 39
Hochbaum, Susan 56, 82
Hough, Jack, Associates 50
Jakob, Robert 88
Jonson Pedersen Hinrichs & Shakery 39
Katz Wheeler Design 71
Laidlaw, Thomas 53
Markey, Lyn 30
Menasion, Charles 71
Miller, Stephen 68
Morin, Tom 50
Oliver, Douglas 24
Ostrie, Barry 10
Pentagram Design 33, 56, 82
Richards, Sullivan, Brock & Associates 42, 68
Robinson, Bennett 13, 22, 47, 62, 74, 85
Runyan, Robert Miles 24, 59, 76
Runyan, Robert Miles, & Associates 24, 59, 76
Saks, Arnold 88
Saks, Arnold, Inc. 88
Schmid, Kaspar 33
Seltzer, Carl 16, 66
Sullivan, Ron 42
Vick, Barbara 39
Weaver, John 36
Weymouth, Michael 30, 53
Weymouth Design 30, 53
Wheeler, Alina R. 71
Zographos, Paula 47, 62, 74, 85

Photographers / Illustrators

Barnett, Peggy 10, 22, 88
Booth, Greg 42, 68
Brady, Carolyn 62
Carroll, Justin 39
Collier, John 62
Cunningham, Robert M. 62
Davidson, Bruce 47, 76, 85
Davis, Paul 62
Donner, Carol 33
Farlow, Melissa 16
Folon, Jean-Michel 62
Fusco, Paul 39
Gaumy, Jean 22
Giusti, Robert 62
Gladstone, Gary 88
Griffiths, Phillip Jones 56
Harrison, Peter 56
Hartig, Karl 33
Hayward, Bill 13
Hess, Mark 19, 33
Hess, Richard 33
Hofer, Evelyn 22
Hollyman, Tom 19
Horowitz, Ryszard 33
Lewis, Stacey 71
Long, Larry 53
Lott, Kip 56
McLean, Wilson 85
McMullan, James 62
Magleby, McRay 42
Meyerson, Arthur 94
Mihaesco, Eugene 33
Mottar, Robert 22
Nelson, Will 39
Newman, Arnold 56
Pacheco, Robert 24
Palmer, Gabe 22
Pannell, Deborah 71
Selkirk, Neil 33
Slavin, Neal 82
Smothers, Bryan 36
Sorel, Edward 62
Steele, Kim 22, 74
Stevens, Robert 59
Tice, George 22
Tracy, Tom 39, 91
Uzzle, Burk 22
Vary, Bill 16
Weaver, Robert 62
Weymouth, Michael 53
Whitmore, Ken 66
Wilcox, David 62

9/Annual Reports

Irving Bank

Because of the more or less intangible nature of their businesses, financial institutions have long found it convenient and efficacious to employ themes of a more or less abstract nature in designing their annual reports. A lending institution, for example, might focus on some of the homes it has mortgaged, while a state bank might explore some of the scenic wonders in its own "backyard."

In its 1982 annual report, the Irving Bank Corporation found apt occasion to develop just such an abstract theme. With the following year being the bicentennial year of the birth of Washington Irving, American author and statesman and the bank's namesake, what could be more fitting, as the report's designer says, than "to pay tribute to Washington Irving and his home, called Sunnyside, in Tarrytown, New York?"

"We wanted to present the Irving home in a special section," continues Barry Ostrie, of John Heiney & Associates, the design firm responsible for the last five Irving Bank reports. "And we wanted to use photography atypical for a 'bank' report, while at the same time retaining design continuity, both in the balance of the report and as compared to previous reports."

But, because of the report's content, there was an additional consideration. For the first time in six years, the bank had experienced a decline in earnings, which were off about 15 per cent from 1981. Obviously, although other aspects of its performance were encouraging, it was no time to issue a spectacular-looking annual.

Irving Bank Corporation 1982 Annual Report

Washington Irving's Home at Sunnyside

By focussing on the life and home of its namesake, Washington Irving, a bank creates a report with both strength and sensitivity.

The low-key treatment of this report creates a mood that is both strong and sensitive. Beyond basic black, the "extra" colors here are two grays, and if it weren't for a few solidly printed pages and some sedately construed bar graphs, the casual reader would not be aware of them.

To the more discerning eye, however, their presence is seen and felt in the three pages of black-and-white photographs accompanying a well-written and eminently readable account of Washington Irving's life. Photographer Peggy Barnett, who is a master of the still life, found a bounty of subjects at Irving's estate—the desk where he wrote his biography of George Washington; some musical instruments; a dressing table; an old cask, splitting at the seams, on the apple-strewn ground near an old stone wall. The glimpses are evocative and personal and, with their regard for light, composition, and form and their excellent reproduction, they establish the report in an atmosphere of balance and thoughtfulness.

Curiously, the effect of this section is felt far beyond the four pages it occupies at the front of the book. The six pages of operations review which follow, set in a reader-sized font of the bank's official Times Roman, seem to flow out of the photo section, even though its unadorned, two-column format has an integrity of its own. And, by the same token, the financial statements, with wide tables and graph-studded commentary, flow from the review.

"The theme of the report was never altered," Ostrie comments, "and the finished

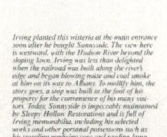
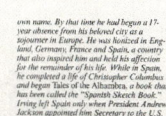

11/Annual Reports

product was precisely what everyone anticipated seeing." And, in a world where design by committee too often prevails, that might have been satisfaction enough.

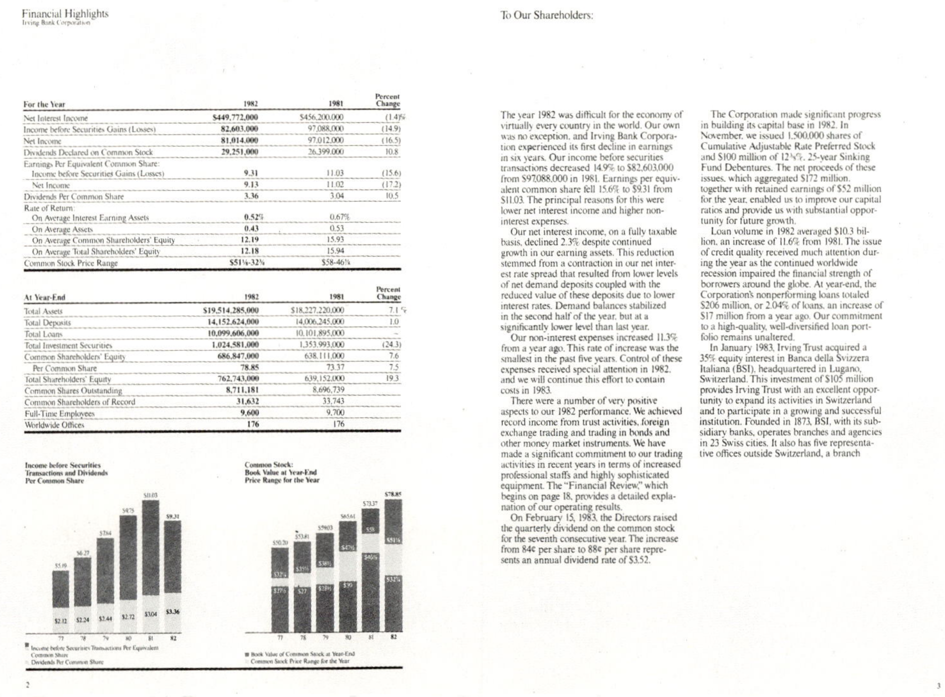

Report: Irving Bank Corporation 1982. Bank holding company. 1982 total assets $19.5 billion.
Design firm: John Heiney & Associates, New York City
Art director/designer: Barry Ostrie
Photographer: Peggy Barnett
Copywriter: Paul Duffy/Irving Bank
Printer: Sanders Printing
Size: 9" by 12"; 58 pages plus covers
Quantity: 95,000

Financial Highlights
Irving Bank Corporation

For the Year	1982	1981	Percent Change
Net Interest Income	$449,772,000	$456,083,000	(1.4)%
Income before Securities Gains (Losses)	82,603,000	97,088,000	(14.9)
Net Income	81,014,000	97,012,000	(16.5)
Dividends Declared on Common Stock	29,251,000	26,399,000	10.8
Earnings Per Equivalent Common Share:			
Income before Securities Gains (Losses)	9.31	11.03	(15.6)
Net Income	9.13	11.02	(17.2)
Dividends Per Common Share	3.36	3.04	10.5
Rate of Return:			
On Average Interest Earning Assets	0.52%	0.67%	
On Average Assets	0.43	0.53	
On Average Common Shareholders' Equity	12.19	15.93	
On Average Total Shareholders' Equity	12.18	15.94	
Common Stock Price Range	$51⅛–32⅜	$58–46⅞	

At Year-End	1982	1981	Percent Change
Total Assets	$19,514,285,000	$18,227,220,000	7.1%
Total Deposits	14,152,624,000	14,006,245,000	1.0
Total Loans	10,099,606,000	10,101,895,000	—
Total Investment Securities	1,024,581,000	1,353,993,000	(24.3)
Common Shareholders' Equity	686,847,000	638,111,000	7.6
Per Common Share	78.85	73.37	7.5
Total Shareholders' Equity	762,743,000	639,152,000	19.3
Common Shares Outstanding	8,711,181	8,696,739	
Common Shareholders of Record	31,632	33,743	
Full-Time Employees	9,600	9,700	
Worldwide Offices	176	176	

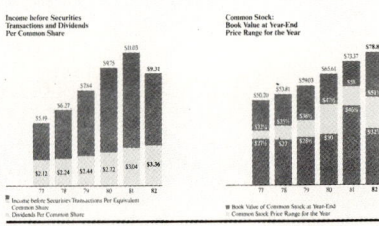

To Our Shareholders:

The year 1982 was difficult for the economy of virtually every country in the world. Our own was no exception, and Irving Bank Corporation experienced its first decline in earnings in six years. Our income before securities transactions decreased 14.9% to $82,603,000 from $97,088,000 in 1981. Earnings per equivalent common share fell 15.6% to $9.31 from $11.03. The principal reasons for this were lower net interest income and higher non-interest expenses.

Our net interest income, on a fully taxable basis, declined 2.3% despite continued growth in our earning assets. This reduction stemmed from a contraction in our net interest rate spread that resulted from lower levels of net demand deposits coupled with the reduced value of these deposits due to lower interest rates. Demand balances stabilized in the second half of the year, but at a significantly lower level than last year.

Our non-interest expenses increased 11.3% from a year ago. This rate of increase was the smallest in the past five years. Control of these expenses received special attention in 1982, and we will continue this effort to contain costs in 1983.

There were a number of very positive aspects to our 1982 performance. We achieved record income from trust activities, foreign exchange trading and trading in bonds and other money market instruments. We have made a significant commitment to our trading activities in recent years in terms of increased professional staffs and highly sophisticated equipment. The "Financial Review" which begins on page 18, provides a detailed explanation of our operating results.

On February 15, 1983, the Directors raised the quarterly dividend on the common stock for the seventh consecutive year. The increase from 84¢ per share to 88¢ per share represents an annual dividend rate of $3.52.

The Corporation made significant progress in building its capital base in 1982. In November, we issued 1,500,000 shares of Cumulative Adjustable Rate Preferred Stock and $100 million of 12⅝%, 25-year Sinking Fund Debentures. The net proceeds of these issues, which aggregated $172 million, together with retained earnings of $52 million for the year, enabled us to improve our capital ratios and provide us with substantial opportunity for future growth.

Loan volume in 1982 averaged $10.3 billion, an increase of 11.6% from 1981. The issue of credit quality received much attention during the year as the continued worldwide recession impaired the financial strength of borrowers around the globe. At year-end, the Corporation's nonperforming loans totaled $206 million, or 2.04% of loans, an increase of $17 million from a year ago. Our commitment to a high-quality, well-diversified loan portfolio remains unaltered.

In January 1983, Irving Trust acquired a 35% equity interest in Banca della Svizzera Italiana (BSI), headquartered in Lugano, Switzerland. This investment of $105 million provides Irving Trust with an excellent opportunity to expand its activities in Switzerland and to participate in a growing and successful institution. Founded in 1873, BSI, with its subsidiary banks, operates branches and agencies in 23 Swiss cities. It also has five representative offices outside Switzerland, a branch

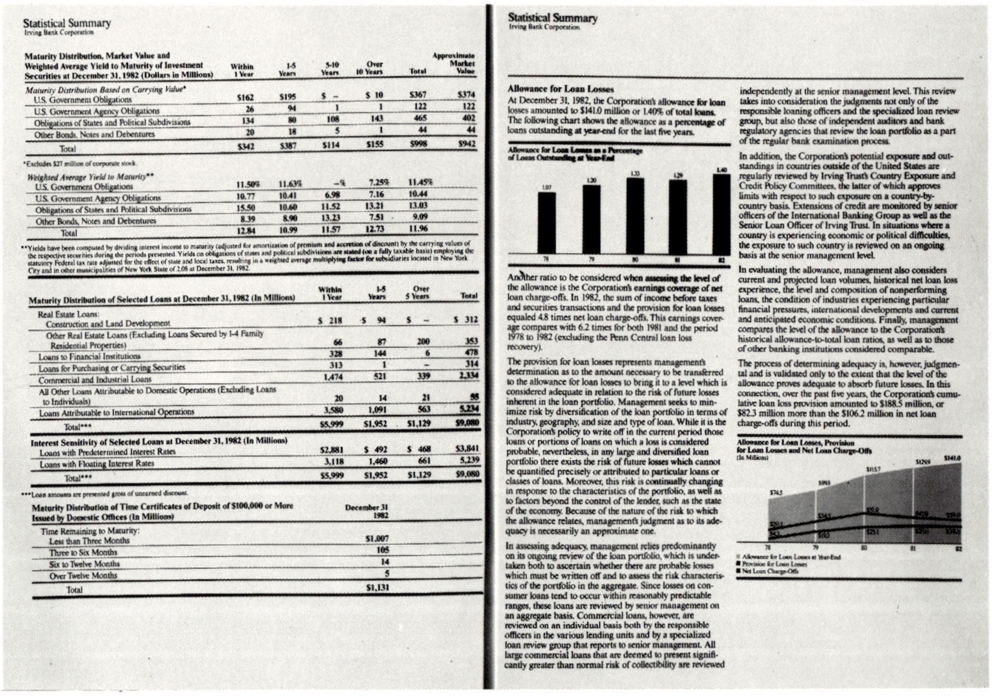

Statistical Summary
Irving Bank Corporation

Maturity Distribution, Market Value and Weighted Average Yield to Maturity of Investment Securities at December 31, 1982 (Dollars in Millions)

	Within 1 Year	1–5 Years	5–10 Years	Over 10 Years	Total	Approximate Market Value
Maturity Distribution Based on Carrying Value*						
U.S. Government Obligations	$162	$195	$ —	$ 10	$367	$374
U.S. Government Agency Obligations	26	94	1	1	122	122
Obligations of States and Political Subdivisions	134	80	108	143	465	402
Other Bonds, Notes and Debentures	20	18	5	1	44	44
Total	$342	$387	$114	$155	$998	$942

*Excludes $27 million of corporate stock.

Weighted Average Yield to Maturity**					
U.S. Government Obligations	11.50%	11.63%	—%	7.25%	11.45%
U.S. Government Agency Obligations	10.77	10.41	6.98	7.16	10.44
Obligations of States and Political Subdivisions	15.50	10.60	11.52	13.21	13.03
Other Bonds, Notes and Debentures	8.39	8.90	13.23	7.51	9.09
Total	12.84	10.99	11.57	12.73	11.96

**Yields have been computed by dividing interest income to maturity (adjusted for amortization of premium and accretion of discount) by the carrying values of the respective securities during the periods presented. Yields on obligations of states and political subdivisions are stated on a fully taxable basis employing the statutory Federal tax rate adjusted for the effect of state and local taxes, resulting in a weighted average multiplying factor for subsidiaries located in New York City and in other municipalities of New York State of 1.08 at December 31, 1982.

Maturity Distribution of Selected Loans at December 31, 1982 (In Millions)

	Within 1 Year	1–5 Years	Over 5 Years	Total
Real Estate Loans:				
Construction and Land Development	$ 218	$ 94	$ —	$ 312
Other Real Estate Loans (Excluding Loans Secured by 1–4 Family Residential Properties)	66	87	200	353
Loans to Financial Institutions	328	144	6	478
Loans for Purchasing or Carrying Securities	313	1	—	314
Commercial and Industrial	1,474	521	339	2,334
All Other Loans Attributable to Domestic Operations (Excluding Loans to Individuals)	20	14	21	55
Loans Attributable to International Operations	3,580	1,091	563	5,234
Total***	$5,999	$1,952	$1,129	$9,080

Interest Sensitivity of Selected Loans at December 31, 1982 (In Millions)

	Within 1 Year	1–5 Years	Over 5 Years	Total
Loans with Predetermined Interest Rates	$2,881	$ 492	$ 468	$3,841
Loans with Floating Interest Rates	3,118	1,460	661	5,239
Total***	$5,999	$1,952	$1,129	$9,080

***Loan amounts are presented gross of unearned discount.

Maturity Distribution of Time Certificates of Deposit of $100,000 or More Issued by Domestic Offices (In Millions)

	December 31 1982
Time Remaining to Maturity:	
Less than Three Months	$1,007
Three to Six Months	105
Six to Twelve Months	14
Over Twelve Months	5
Total	$1,131

Statistical Summary
Irving Bank Corporation

Allowance for Loan Losses
At December 31, 1982, the Corporation's allowance for loan losses amounted to $141.0 million or 1.40% of total loans. The following chart shows the allowance as a percentage of loans outstanding at year-end for the last five years.

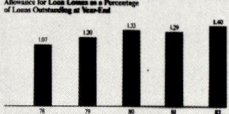

Another ratio to be considered when assessing the level of the allowance is the Corporation's earnings coverage of net loan charge-offs. In 1982, the sum of income before taxes and securities transactions and the provision for loan losses equaled 4.8 times net loan charge-offs. This earnings coverage compares with 6.2 times for both 1981 and the period 1978 to 1982 (excluding the Penn Central loan loss recovery).

The provision for loan losses represents management's determination as to the amount necessary to be transferred to the allowance for loan losses to bring it to a level which is considered adequate in relation to the risk of future losses inherent in the loan portfolio. Management seeks to minimize risk by diversification of the loan portfolio in terms of industry, geography, and size and type of loan. While it is the Corporation's policy to write off in the current period those loans or portions of loans on which a loss is considered probable, nevertheless, in any large and diversified loan portfolio there exists the risk of future losses which cannot be quantified precisely or attributed to particular loans or classes of loans. Moreover, this risk is continually changing in response to the characteristics of the portfolio, as well as to factors beyond the control of the lender, such as the state of the economy. Because of the nature of the risk to which the allowance relates, management's judgment as to its adequacy is necessarily an approximate one.

In assessing adequacy, management relies predominantly on its ongoing review of the loan portfolio, which is undertaken both to ascertain whether there are probable losses which must be written off and to assess the risk characteristics of the portfolio in the aggregate. Since losses on consumer loans tend to occur within reasonably predictable ranges, these loans are reviewed by senior management on an aggregate basis. Commercial loans, however, are reviewed on an individual basis both by the responsible officers in the various lending units and by a specialized loan review group that reports to senior management. All large commercial loans that are deemed to present significantly greater than normal risk of collectibility are reviewed independently at the senior management level. This review takes into consideration the judgments not only of the responsible loaning officers and the specialized loan review group, but also those of independent auditors and bank regulatory agencies that review the loan portfolio as a part of the regular bank examination process.

In addition, the Corporation's potential exposure and outstandings in countries outside of the United States are regularly reviewed by Irving Trust's Country Exposure and Credit Policy Committees, the latter of which approves limits with respect to such countries. Extensions of credit are monitored by senior officers of the International Banking Group as well as the Senior Loan Officer of Irving Trust. In situations where a country is experiencing economic or political difficulties, the exposure to such country is reviewed on an ongoing basis at the senior management level.

In evaluating the allowance, management also considers current and projected loan volumes, historical net loan loss experience, the level and composition of nonperforming loans, the condition of industries experiencing particular financial pressures, international developments and current and anticipated economic conditions. Finally, management compares the level of the allowance to the Corporation's historical allowance-to-total loan ratios, as well as to those of other banking institutions considered comparable.

The process of determining adequacy is, however, judgmental and is validated only to the extent that the level of the allowance proves adequate to absorb future losses. In this connection, over the past five years, the Corporation's cumulative loan loss provision amounted to $188.5 million, or $82.3 million more than the $106.2 million in net loan charge-offs during this period.

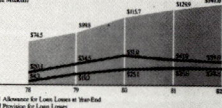

Management Assistance, Inc.

Annual report watchers have come to expect a certain vernacular in the design of reports for computer-involved businesses: the glossy, full-color photography of employees developing or assembling the products, the ever-present user seated in front of the CRT. The accent is high-tech, with enough people visible to remind the reader that computers are, after all, sophisticated *human* tools.

The report designed by Corporate Graphics for Management Assistance, Inc. (MAI) in 1982 sought to break out of this mold. "It's the first humanized computer manufacturer report I've seen," says its art director/designer, Bennett Robinson, "and that's just what we set out to do. Most people are intimidated by computers, when what they're for is to help people. This report shows people just like you and me who were helped by MAI's computer systems."

The emphasis here is decidedly human. In the whole of the operations review, there is not one photo of a computer—in fact, this section has no pictures at all except for a discreetly proportioned, mezzo-tinted halftone of one of the company's latest ideas—a computer "service station" for small computer users. Tucked neatly away toward the back of the report and flowing uninterruptedly into the financial statements, this section is a straightforward account of MAI's business year, set in wide columns (one to a page) and highlighted with simple horizontal bar graphs printed in earthy tones.

The stress on the human element—and the

Management Assistance Inc.
1982 Annual Report

photography—is confined to the front of the report and begins with a silhouetted black-and-white photo of the chairman and president perched on a pedestal table next to a computer console. Here, we see, is a regular guy—a half-smiling, friendly face, somebody's brother-in-law—perfectly at ease with his computer. The effect is disarming, and prepares us for what is to come.

The second of the book's only two computer pictures follows—on the opening page of the special "solutions" section, which aims to show other people-like-us and how they found relative happiness through MAI systems. "For managers to make appropriate business decisions," the theme statement tells us, "vast quantities of information must be processed rapidly and efficiently and must be readily available in manageable form." The accompanying black-and-white photo, again silhouetted, shows MAI's basic means for managing this kind of information.

What follows are nine case histories, run in italics in blue, with a few words in black leading into each story. All of the photos here are black-and-white; some are silhouetted, with text running around their variously shaped edges; some are run square and full frame, with black borders intact. For each, an MAI client was invited to New York City to be photographed in the studio of photographer Bill Hayward and while some are pictured with business-related props (a manufacturer of aluminum window frames looks through one at the camera; the maker

of swiveling easy chairs sits reading in one; a doctor wears white lab coat and stethoscope), none of these are computers.

"The computer is as necessary and as familiar as the telephone and the typewriter," Robinson says. "They don't dazzle us anymore. So we wanted to stress the human dimension by picturing only the people who use them."

The approach is effective. The decision to use black-and-white photography in itself might have served to deglamorize a technology-based report; and black-and-white photography of people, especially in a more or less documentary style, has always held a good deal of credibility.

From a design viewpoint, the low-keyed photography and colored text fit nicely with other aspects of the production. The cover and non-photograph pages (except for that one mezzotint) are of a high-finish, soft white Mohawk Superfine; the photo section is on Cameo Gloss.

This slicker sheet is also printed solid black as a divider page introducing the operations/financial review, and on its reverse side is a studio shot of MAI's management committee. Standing around on the photographer's no-seam with their hands in their pockets, these MAI senior officers have been demystified, de-formalized, and made men; in short, they emerge, like the chairman, as people like us.

An unusual report for a computer company shuns hardware and color photography to portray—in black-and-white—some users of the company's products.

Report: Management Assistance, Inc. 1982. Information processing systems and maintenance services. 1982 revenues $358 million.
Design firm: Corporate Graphics, New York City
Art director: Bennett Robinson
Designers: Bennett Robinson, Naomi Burstein
Copywriter: Harvey Shapiro
Photographer: Bill Hayward
Printer: The Hennegan Co.
Size: 8½" by 11"; 50 pages plus covers
Quantity: 70,000

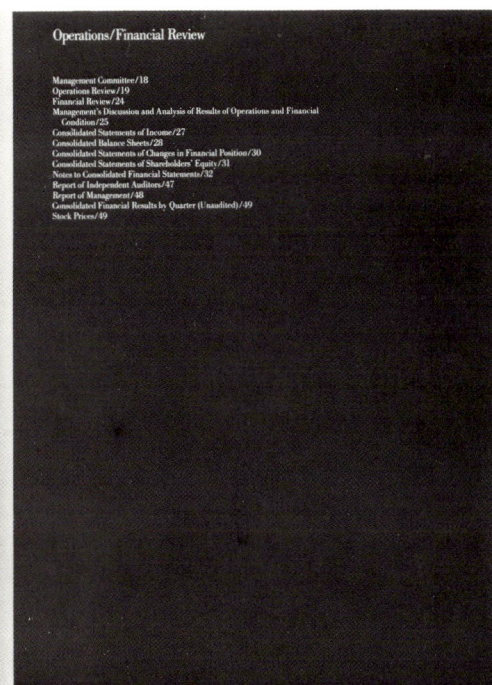

15/Annual Reports

Northrop

The Northrop Corporation is one of a handful whose annual reports are habitual winners in Casebook competitions. Their design is notable for a level of taste and consistency not often seen in annual reports (or elsewhere, for that matter), and their story is all the more interesting because, for the past several years, they have been produced exclusively in black-and-white.

That a single West Coast design firm, Cross Associates, has produced 20 Northrop reports, and that the one shown here, as well as the four previous reports, were designed by the same man—Carl Seltzer—no doubt has contributed a great deal to their cohesiveness. But at the same time, Northrop is a strong organization in itself whose current image has been molded by a singular vision—that of Les Daly, Northrop vice president for public affairs.

It was Daly who moved Northrop's reports from color to black-and-white when he joined the firm a number of years ago, and far from thinking of the annual report as the generator of an image, he sees Northrop's black-and-white report as being the outcome of what the company does.

"We are in the defense business," Daly has said. "It doesn't deal in flashy, colorful products—it's a very serious business. It's natural to do our annual report in black-and-white—it's a matter of who we are."

Daly, moreover, not only oversees the production of the report; he has a firm hand in its development from the ground up—from selecting the photographer and photographs

Annual Reports/16

to choosing papers and highlight colors. All members of the report team, from writer to printer, are responsible directly to him.

The design of the company's 1981 report was effected around a particular problem: the inclusion in the report of a photograph of a fighter plane, the F-5G Tigershark, which Northrop had taken the initiative in developing and marketing on its own. The photograph was to appear as a double-page spread—and it was to be in color—a real departure for Northrop reports.

Now, for some time, "black-and-white" in Northrop books has meant scanned-duotone or tritone printing for halftones, and another color or two used for heads, rules, or other highlights. In the case of the 1981 report, these colors—a rich red and a sky blue—were selected to correspond to the predominant colors in the Tigershark photo. The red was used in highlight statements and bolder rules, and the blue was barely visible hairlines.

The operations portion of the report flows through the front of the book, where sensitively composed black-and-white photographs fill the left-hand portions of the spreads. Through this section, as well as the letter to shareholders, the Tigershark is discussed matter-of-factly, as Northrop discusses any of its programs or operations. It is only at page 27—a black divider page printed in red and blue—that we get a hint of something special, and, turning the divider, we see the plane: a red, white, and blue silhouette against a blackened sky. (The whole shot was a set-up, of

17/Annual Reports

course, but nonetheless impressive.)

Interestingly, this one color reproduction doesn't jar the senses. Its colors are so muted that we hardly think of it as being in color at all, and the careful selecting of highlight colors for the rest of the book camouflages its presence. Somehow, like the use of black-and-white by Northrop for the annual report as a whole, this picture seems a very natural conclusion.

Report: Northrop Corporation 1981. Aerospace design, engineering, and fabrication and related systems, instruments, and services. 1981 sales $1.99 billion.
Design firm: Cross Associates, Los Angeles
Art director: James Cross
Designer: Carl Seltzer
Photographers: Melissa Farlow (major photography), Bill Vary
Copywriters: Les Daly, Greg Waskul/Northrop
Printer: Gardner/Fullmer
Size: 8½" by 11"; 56 pages plus covers
Quantity: 77,000

A predominantly black-and-white report continues this Northrop tradition while taking its cue from a single full-color image: a striking view of Northrop's own F-5G Tigershark (above).

Annual Reports/18

Champion International

One of the advantages of the Casebook series is that, while it offers an overview of the development of graphic design trends, it also lets the reader see, in the case of repeat winners, how one particular client or designer meets through time the challenges of a changing marketplace.

Nowhere is this more apparent than in the case of annual reports, and when that client and designer are a team that has for years relied on more or less the same annual report design to weather any economic clime, the case is particularly interesting—and particularly challenging.

The solution to the problems confronting Champion International in putting together their 1981 annual report was essentially one developed by their designer, Richard Hess, in 1974. At that time, Champion had been undergoing some drastic changes in management strategies, and the strict stylizing of the report—which was to endure for five years—was seen as a stabilizing measure.

In terms of corporate image, the report has become more than that. The format was so successful that it is still in use, and may well be for years to come, for its identifiable and recognizable format has kept Champion's corporate image riding high through all sorts of economic lows.

The 1981 Champion report, which appears here, is the second issued since designer Hess started revamping (ever so slightly) his time-honored design in 1980. That year, he replaced the corporation's symbol, traditionally embossed on the cover, with an

Another highly formatted Champion report continues the new cover treatment begun in 1980—the life cycle of a tree.

19/Annual Reports

embossed, full-color painting of the life cycle of a tree. The second change that year, a seemingly small one, was more far-reaching: He replaced the corporate, Helvetica typeface—which had been used through the report—with a more readable Garamond.

While these changes seemed at first superficial, one sees, looking back, that they signalled a shift in emphasis for both Champion and the use to which the company had put its annual report. The strict format of earlier reports had done its job, had imparted the stabilizing image. Now, the corporation could afford to relax its visual stance, to open its report to other messages and other means.

The 1981 report bears this out. While the report obviously seeks to provide analysts and stockholders with hard-core financial information, says Champion annual report coordinator Mary E. Green, the report also sought "to appeal to the casual reader with a clearly stated 'picture' of the corporation and its operations."

The picture on its traditionally die-cut cover—a Douglas fir—is a direct link to the loblolly pine which appeared on the previous report, and to the botanical basis of the company's business. The photo spreads, which again alternate with spreads of text running within divisions along operational lines, are captioned by up-sized, medium-gray copy blocks which say more about Champion's business practices than about the particular picture.

On text pages we find the graphic devices Champion report-watchers are by now

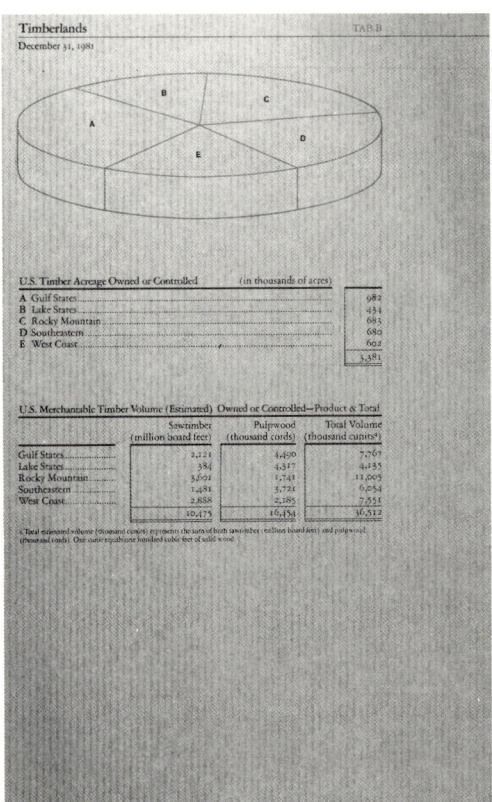

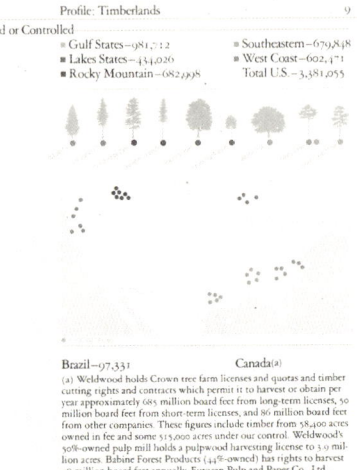

familiar with: tree silhouettes (here in gray), stylized operations maps (gray with colored dots), schematics (explaining manufacturing processes), and small but colorful graphs and charts that keep text lively and interesting and the whole book fresh and appealing. Divider pages are again Carnival Groove (khaki), but, in deference to a downturn in operations results, the paper mix is a conservative three (there were five in 1980), and there are no embossings or fold-outs as in other, more prosperous years.

For designer Hess, it is production variations like these, as well as a constantly renewable mix of design elements, which makes each formatted report unique. "Working within this size and shape," he says, "I could probably do new designs for the next 20 years. The only problem I have is the problem of content. Champion's business remains the same year after year, and it's a manufacturing story. It becomes difficult: How many ways can you show a paper machine so that you're not showing the same picture you did last year?"

Report: Champion International 1981. Building materials, pulp and paper, packaging. 1981 sales $4 billion.
Design firm: Richard Hess, Inc., Roxbury, CT
Art director/designer: Richard Hess
Photographer: Tom Hollyman
Illustrator: Mark Hess
Copywriters: Patricia L. Stoddard, David R. Brown/Champion
Printer: Case-Hoyt
Size: 7" by 11"; 66 pages plus dividers and covers
Quantity: 110,000

Building Products 20

Housing Depression Hammers Wood Businesses——For the past two years, rising interest and mortgage rates, spiraling costs of new houses, and declining economic health have combined to drive the housing industry into its longest and deepest slump since 1946. While our sales of building materials slipped slightly in 1981, earnings from operations—including the wood products segment of our Weldwood of Canada subsidiary—were hammered to their lowest levels on record. Canadian markets for building materials were mixed until the third quarter of 1981, when an industry-wide strike in British Columbia plus faltering world economic conditions produced a major fall-off in both Canadian and export sales.

By the time the U.S. economy officially entered a recession in the second half of 1981, the rapid escalation in housing prices had begun to ease, and mortgage rates began to decline bit by bit. At year's end, however, the home building industry was still under siege. Other markets for Champion's wood products—such as furniture and fixtures, mobile homes, remodeling and alterations, for example—are basically sensitive either to housing or general economic activity, and during 1981 both suffered. Forecasts vary widely as to the availability of mortgage money and the likely levels of interest rates—both critical to our wood products businesses—over the next 12 months.

Managing in a Catastrophe——During the course of this grim year, sales volume held up reasonably well largely due to the exemplary performance of our sales and distribution system. Our mills, though curtailed from time to time, ran at an operating rate ahead of the industry, and in terms of labor productivity and log recovery they performed very well.

However, lumber and plywood were selling for less than

Building Products 21

their 1979 prices, and the timber industry generally experienced its worst markets since World War II. It was the low prices that caused the agony and the sharp earnings decline.

In the face of these unprecedented market conditions, we took our inventories down to an absolute minimum and tightened up on our receivables. We trimmed costs all down the line, and deferred capital spending. Where possible, we shifted products around toward do-it-yourself and industrial markets, and throughout all of this our manufacturing productivity went up.

Curtailments, however, were necessary and decisions as to when and where to curtail became a matter of determining the effect of a closure on our whole system—both on building products facilities and on chip supplies to paper and packaging mills. As the solid wood converting arm of Champion's integrated forest products business, the building products plants are a key link in the fiber procurement system for many of our pulp mills and enable the company to make optimum use of fee and contract timber.

Ongoing Modernization Program——In an important effort to capture the most product and most profit from every tree, we have spent $225 million during the past five years on modernization, expan-

sion programs, and operations maintenance at our domestic lumber and plywood facilities. We expect to spend nearly $250 million during the next five years in continued support of these domestic operations. An additional $180 million is planned for the solid wood operations of Weldwood of Canada. For the time being, however, programs in both domestic and Canadian operations are basically on hold. Once reactivated, these programs will further our aim to improve on Champion's position as one of the most cost-effective producers of building materials in the industry. For example, major modernization projects will continue at the Roseburg, Oregon, facility and the Newberry, South Carolina, plant. A developmental program in recovery improvement utilizing advanced technology is under way at our Corrigan, Texas, plywood plant.

The Outlook——Champion should emerge from this housing depression among the strongest of the survivors—leaner, more productive, and more cost-competitive. In addition to improving our mar-

Although the last two years of depression in the housing industry may have changed many things, one that has not changed—and cannot change—is the demographic pressure for new houses. Demographics? A statistical study of the American population reveals that some 59 million people, or 26 percent of our total society, are now between 20 and 34 years of age. In the past, that's when people bought their first houses. Now and in the future, the demand for housing will continue to be insistent. Some think housing in the U.S. has gone way beyond an issue of economics and may become one of the key domestic political and social issues of the 1980s.

21/Annual Reports

Automatic Data Processing

Like the report for Management Assistance, discussed earlier in this book, Automatic Data Processing's (ADP's) 1981 annual report breaks away from the high-tech emphasis so often associated with companies in the computer business. And, like that report, this one also makes major use of black-and-white photography to impart a particular message.

But for ADP, the message—and the organization of the report—is altogether different. The emphasis here is on markets and on meeting their needs through ADP's 32 increasingly successful years, and all other, more conventional front-of-the-book data has been subordinated to this communications goal.

The report opens with a highlights table, followed by the letter to shareholders. Not merely a recapitulation of an operations text, this letter actually incorporates the information normally reserved for a business-by-business review. And since ADP has only one business—providing data-processing services—the major portion of the book is given over to an examination of the markets for those services.

For this discussion, which has been divided into five topical essays, copy pages of a buff-colored Strathmore Artlaid sheet have been interleaved with pages of dull-finished Quintessence. Accompanying the ragged-right, Bembo text are small vertical bar graphs, which are printed in earthy red and ochre in the pages' broad outer margins. The gloss sheet opposite each bears a single, modestly scaled black-and-white photograph researched from various sources; this

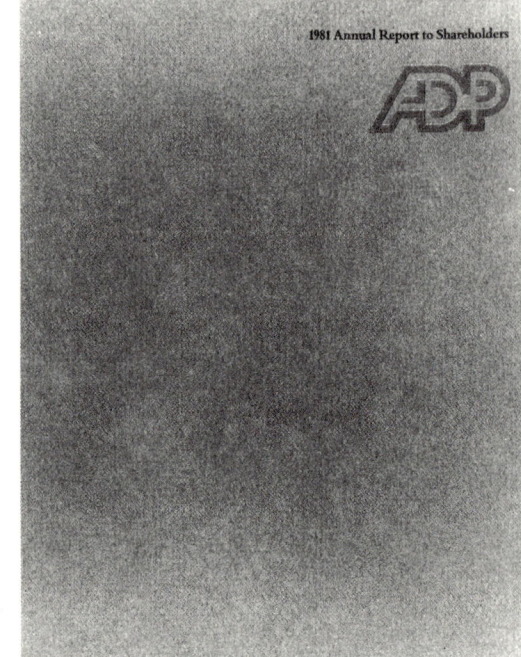

A conservative report for a computer services organization emphasizes the historical needs of business and contrasts them with contemporary ways to meet them.

Annual Reports/22

photo is directly linked with the market being discussed in the text.

Ranging from the curious to the dramatic, these timeless images—and the captions accompanying them—might have remained the only visualization of ADP's businesses. But, art director Bennett Robinson tells us, toward the end of the production phase, ADP management asked to have some of the company's timely solutions to these timeless problems also incorporated into the report.

Robinson responded by hiring photographer Gabe Palmer to make color photographs of various ADP processors. Sized barely larger than postage stamps, one of these was tucked beneath each black-and-white image, and, despite their scale, tight cropping and close-up imaging renders each easily readable. Moreover, they offer neat visual counterpoint to the little bar graphs on the text pages, since the graphs are approximately the same size.

Report: Automatic Data Processing, Inc. 1981. Computing services. 1981 revenues $558 million.
Design firm: Corporate Graphics, Inc., New York City
Art director: Bennett Robinson
Designer: James Hatch
Photographers: Gabe Palmer (color); Peggy Barnett, Robert Mottar/Chase Manhattan Archives, Burk Uzzle/Magnum, Evelyn Hofer, George Tice, Kim Steele, Jean Gaumy/Magnum
Copywriter: Automatic Data Processing
Printer: Anderson Lithography
Size: 8½" by 10½"; 36 pages plus covers
Quantity: 105,000

Financial institutions are undergoing rapid change with electronic payment systems supplementing traditional methods. ADP is in the forefront of practical technology and offers such services as Pay-by-Phone and ATM networks to client institutions.

The securities industry is among the most information-intensive of modern business activities and is a major ADP market. ADP services increase the productivity of brokerage firms, improve their ability to serve customers and provide instantaneous market information.

23/Annual Reports

Orthopaedic Hospital

While such organizations as private partnerships, hospitals, and operating foundations are not governed by the same financial reporting laws as publicly-held corporations, they generally do issue yearly (or perhaps bi- or tri-yearly) accountings of their revenues and expenses. And, while many of these reports are verbal rather than visual exercises, more and more are speaking the language of the contemporary corporate report—and being recognized in the major collections of well-designed annual reports.

Two such, for Los Angeles' Orthopaedic Hospital, were designed by the office of Robert Miles Runyan, a firm instrumental in creating the modern annual report style. And differences in rules and regulations notwithstanding, the problems posed in creating these reports were not too different from those faced in designing any corporate review: to present the organization as technologically sophisticated, without sacrificing the element of human warmth.

For both of these reports, dated 1981 and 1982, the budget was a critical consideration—no more than 50 cents per copy for 1981, and less for '82. In both years, the report was designed around strong black-and-white photography and tailored to meet the demands of the particular year.

In 1981, hospital management wished to emphasize its technological expertise. Founded in 1922, Orthopaedic Hospital was conceived to provide treatment for physically disabled children whose families could not afford private care. Since that time, some of the

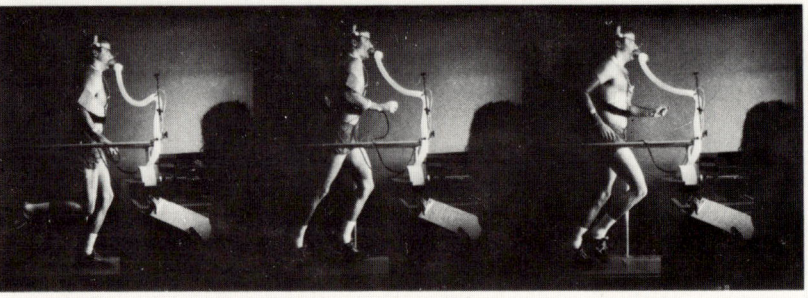

1981 Annual Report

problems the hospital sought to combat have all but disappeared. In addition, methods of diagnosis and treatment have changed dramatically, and the hospital, among the most advanced orthopedic centers in the western U.S., wished to position itself at the leading edge of medical technology.

The designers met these needs with a clean, straightforward solution that combines the look of a black-and-white proof sheet with a Bodoni running text and plenty of white space. Set in horizontal sequences of four, the photo-frames are reminiscent of the motion studies made by Eadweard Muybridge, especially the report's cover strip, which pictures a man jogging on a treadmill, his head and body wired to a computer that will assess the performance of his heart and lungs.

The format ran into two obstacles during design and production. The first came with a directive from the president of the hospital to show both new construction and new hospital programs, the two of which were visually unrelated. The problem was resolved by photographing the construction site in the same vein as the "action" sequences. Where the subject is static, the camera moves across it, creating a sense of movement for the reader as his eyes scan the various views. In both cases, the photo-strips are active and engaging.

The second problem arose during the shooting of photographs. The design format called for the "contact prints" to string together

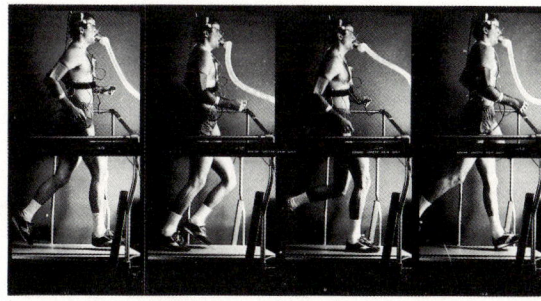

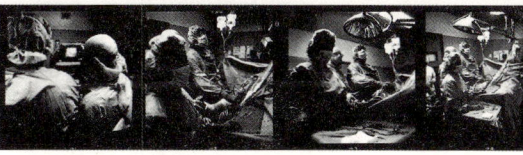

25/Annual Reports

horizontally, but the 2¼" camera strung them vertically. "We'd decided that we wanted the frames to be real sequences," says the report's art director, Bob Runyan; "therefore, the Kodak frame numbers had to be legible and real on the frame edges. So we rented an eyepiece that enabled us to shoot with the Hasselblad turned on its side at a 90-degree angle. This made the resulting negative strips horizontal rather than vertical."

The following year, the report was asked to communicate the message of leadership, but on a smaller budget. As a result, the designers decreased the number of pages from 24 (including self-cover) to 16. In addition, the overall trim size of the book was made considerably smaller to reflect the proportions of the photography, which was run one picture across a double-page spread; this design decision also effected a savings in paper.

The Orthopaedic Hospital 1982 report, in relying on a more human emphasis, presents the case histories of four individuals, hospital patients who, as the report's introduction tells us, "have in common remarkable courage and dignity in their struggle to overcome a disability." Their stories are moving, indeed: one young woman, who has been a victim of rheumatoid arthritis since childhood, remarks, "Me and pain are old friends"; another, a two-year-old who suffered brain damage at birth, now has cerebral palsy and little chance for a normal life. (This tot smiles at us from his mother's arms, and we realize

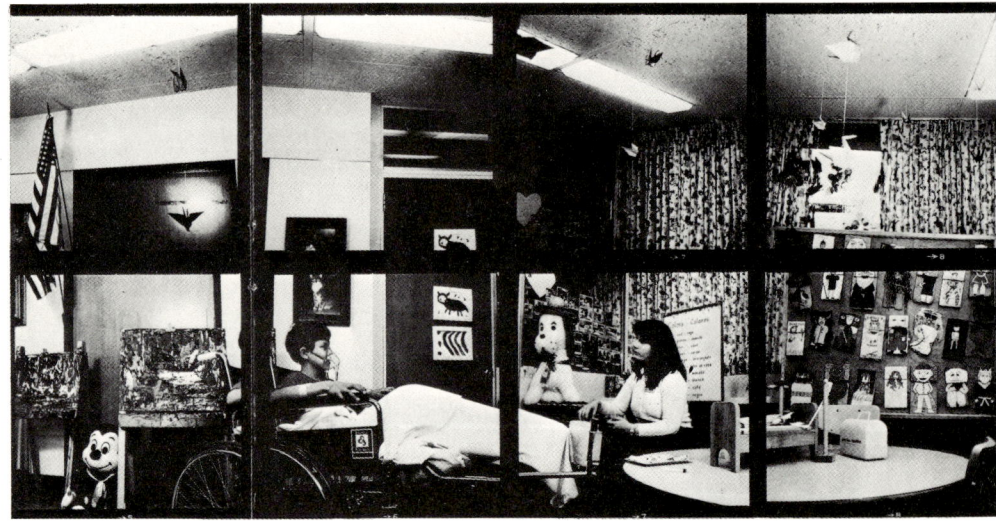

Two black-and-white reports for a hospital focus on advanced technology and the needs of people . . .

that the case history is as much about her courage and suffering as it is about his.)

Visually, this report is as strong as, or stronger than, the previous one, despite corner-cutting. The photo blow-ups, which place the subject in the right-hand portion of the frame, are cropped with their black borders intact (including frame numbers) and bleeding off the edges of the spread. The case history text, as well as a close-up of the face of the individual, are positioned in the left-hand portion of the frame and seem to float before the white no-seam backdrop against which the patients are posed. The overall crisp black-and-white format with pictures by the same photographer, Robert Pacheco, and the black photo borders are a direct allusion to the previous year's report, and they create a strong sense of continuity.

In addition to the tri-tone process used for photographic reproduction, both books employ a double hit of a PMS color—bright yellow in 1981, sky blue in 1982. The colors form a backdrop to introductory copy (inside front cover and page one) and financial copy and supply a minimum of spot color in the photo section of each report.

The nature of the textual presentation of financial data, while not a matter of graphic design, also deserves a note. In accounting for revenues and expenditures, bold-faced taglines lead the reader through the tables of items and figures ("We charged the following for patient services. . .but because of care provided to [various non-paying patients, with deficits in dollar amounts], the

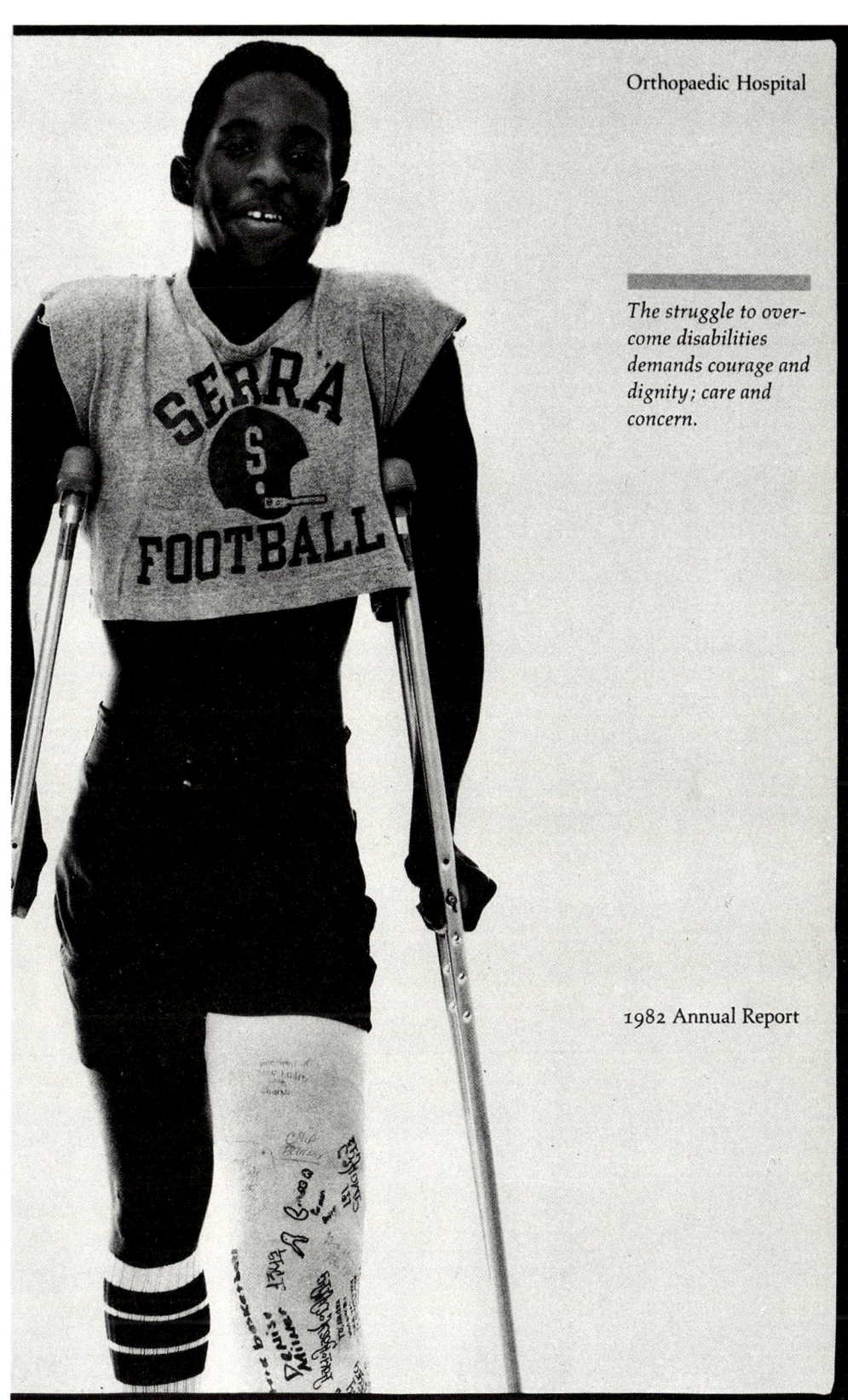

Orthopaedic Hospital

The struggle to overcome disabilities demands courage and dignity; care and concern.

1982 Annual Report

27/Annual Reports

net amount earned from patients was. . ."). The format is unusual, and certainly not the kind of thing one finds in an SEC report. But for those without degrees in accounting, or the just plain uninitiated, this kind of financial interpretation in plain English makes a good deal of sense.

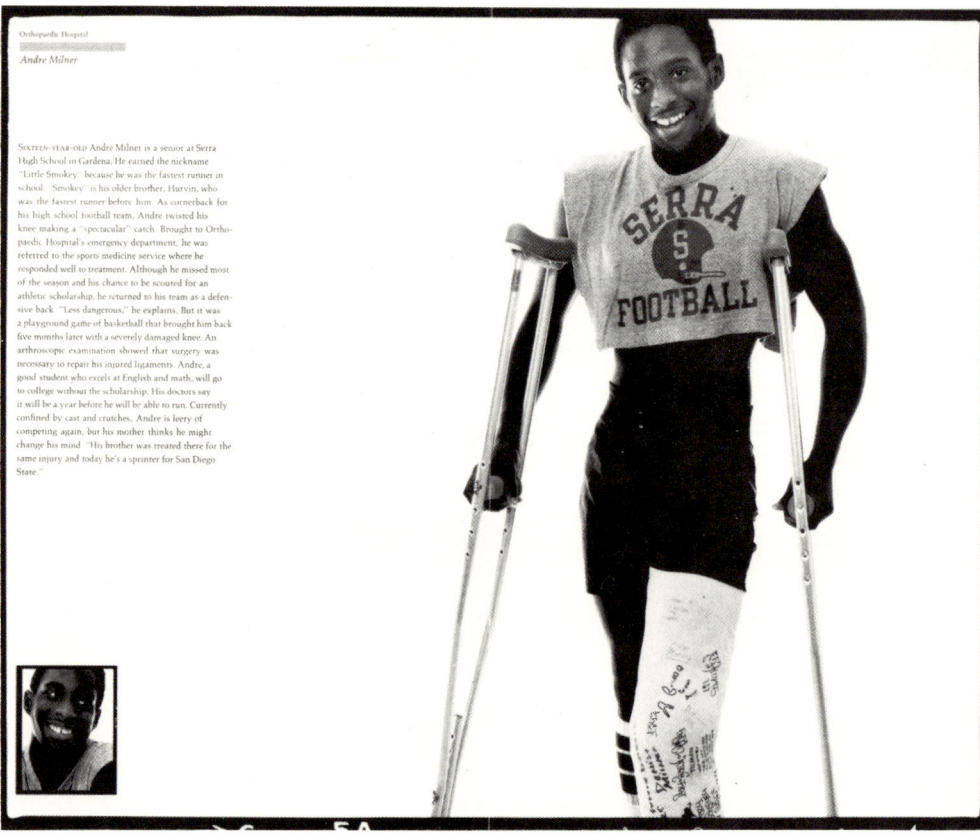

Report: Orthopaedic Hospital 1981 and 1982. Orthopedic medicine and surgery. 1981 revenues $26 million; 1982 revenues $31 million.
Design firm: Robert Miles Runyan and Associates, Los Angeles
Art director: Robert Miles Runyan
Designer: Douglas Oliver
Photographer: Robert Pacheco
Copywriter: Anita Bennett/ Orthopaedic Hospital
Printer: George Rice & Sons
Size: 8½" by 11", 24 pages self-cover (1981); 7" by 11", 16 pages self-cover (1982)
Quantity: 65,000

Annual Reports/28

Orthopaedic Hospital

Janice Foxworth

"Me and pain are old friends," says Janice Foxworth, talking about her longtime battle with rheumatoid arthritis, a chronic, debilitating disease that does not limit itself to the elderly. Janice has been a patient at Orthopaedic Hospital since she was 12 years old. Treated first in the juvenile rheumatoid arthritis service, she is now, at 21, a patient in the adult service. She said her doctor sent her to Orthopaedic because he had helped her all he could. Janice underwent painful treatment to straighten her knees — they were locked in a curved position due to damage caused by her arthritis. "I hated it here. I knew they were going to stick pins in me," she says. She was hospitalized in hinged casts for five weeks, and each day the bolts of the hinges were tightened to straighten her knees. Released from the hospital, she wore plastic splints and walked with crutches. For a year, she was confined to a wheelchair. Today, with knees still somewhat bent, Janice walks without any appliances or aids. She has had extensive physical therapy and was taught to swim by hospital therapists. Graduated from Loyola Marymount High School, Janice attended business college and is working while going to school at night. She hopes to study psychology. "I set goals for myself. I wanted to buy a car and so I got this job to pay for it. Now I'm not afraid of needles or the hospital. I don't like having to come — I'm not crazy, but I'm not afraid. Everyone here knows me and everyone still treats me super sweet, even after all I've put them through." Janice's doctors have recommended surgery to replace her damaged knees; she has declined, explaining that, for now, she has had enough pain. "I don't want it now. Except for my arthritis, I'm in good shape. I want to change my job and continue my education."

. . . and create a sensitive portrait of a hospital that cares.

29/Annual Reports

Compo Industries

The American footwear industry has been going through some troubled times. Despite increases in sales and number of retail outlets selling footwear, increasingly fewer of these sales have been of footwear domestically produced. While costs of raw materials are more or less uniform worldwide, lower costs for labor outside the U.S. enable footwear produced abroad to be imported here and sold at a significantly lower price to the consumer.

Effecting a strong position for a supplier of materials, chemicals, equipment, and services to this sagging industry is indeed a challenge. Yet, through cooperation of client, public relations counsel, and design team, Compo Industries has done just that with its 1982 annual report.

"Newsome and Company, Compo's PR firm, suggested a 'white paper' on the issues and opportunities in the footwear business," explains the report's art director, Mike Weymouth of Weymouth Design in Boston. "This allowed a framework around which Compo's footwear business—as well as its diversified non-footwear business—would fit."

For the designers, however, the major challenge lay in the time allowed them to produce the report. They were called in only two weeks before the client's September 30 year-end, and had only three months to design and produce the report.

From the art director's view, there were two factors which seem to have eased the time crunch. One was that, although Compo is a "last-minute company," once they get started, they "bring all of their

forces to bear." The other factor was that Weymouth is himself an annual report photographer *par excellence.*

Weymouth began the job by spending a few days at Compo making photographs, then pulling together layouts based on those shots. But as the report deadline approached, Compo's thinking became more and more refined, in order to reflect the president's vision of the company. Alterations were made, and Weymouth followed up with additional shooting.

"One of the problems with any company," Weymouth notes, "is that, while they want to look different each year, a designer/photographer can only go so far if the time is limited. The various pressures tend to push all things into dead center. As a result, Compo's president, Leonard Rosenblatt, wanted things revised because they 'looked like last year's report.' His requests were not creatively unreasonable—just hard to deal with within the schedule."

Two areas of difficulty included the "white paper" section and the cover of the report. The former was positioned in the front of the book, immediately following the highlights and letter to shareholders. Printed in five PMS colors (black, green, blue, and two grays) on a soft gray text stock, the straightforward essay section was dramatized by a series of graphs that were consistent with its no-nonsense content. This section was modified a few times to bring content and presentation together.

The cover was also produced in three versions. Besides the one used, Weymouth shot a

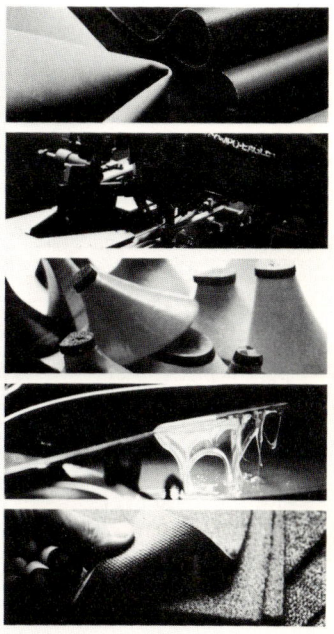

A shoe manufacturer uses its annual report to issue a "white paper" on the state of the nation's shoe business.

31/Annual Reports

variation using magnetic tape instead of punch (because, Weymouth says, the former is "more state-of-the-art"), and another with computer-generated artwork instead of a computer print-out. The final version was selected because it most clearly represented the idea of computer technology being applied in the shoe-manufacturing industry.

Amazingly, Weymouth reports, despite pressures of time and changes made by the client, his original concept for the report remained intact, and this for him was particularly satisfying. "This job had the potential to fly apart at any moment," he says. "It was terrific to feel the heat of the kitchen and still hold it all together."

Report: Compo Industries, Inc. 1982. Materials, chemicals, equipment, and services to the footwear and other industries. 1982 sales $106 million.
Design firm: Weymouth Design, Boston
Art director/photographer: Mike Weymouth
Designer: Lyn Markey
Copywriter: Compo Industries
Printer: Daniels Printing
Size: 8½" by 11"; 40 pages plus covers
Quantity: 15,000

Annual Reports/32

Drexel Burnham Lambert

In an effort to expand the boundaries of what might be called the typically well-designed modern annual report, designers have been experimenting with new and different ways to couch the corporate message. One of these, which keeps reappearing from time to time, is the magazine format, and if many past efforts left something to be desired, the jurors for this Casebook found the Drexel Burnham Lambert 1982 annual review a particularly well-executed example of the form.

And in adapting any form to another purpose, execution is of the essence. "The concept was to use a magazine format," says Colin Forbes of Pentagram Design, who art-directed the book, "and with that idiom, to comment on financial issues. We felt the quality and style of the photography and illustration should be equal to the best monthly magazines."

Drexel Burnham Lambert (DBL) is a New York-based investment research and financial services firm with offices here and abroad, and while investment research forms the cornerstone of DBL's business, the firm also counsels individual and institutional investors, provides underwriting and market-making for bonds and securities, and has dealings in commodities, real estate, investment banking, and public finance.

"The objective of DBL's communication program," says Forbes, "is to position the firm as a leader in the securities industry and as an interpreter of economic trends. The editorial matter and the design of their 1982 annual review

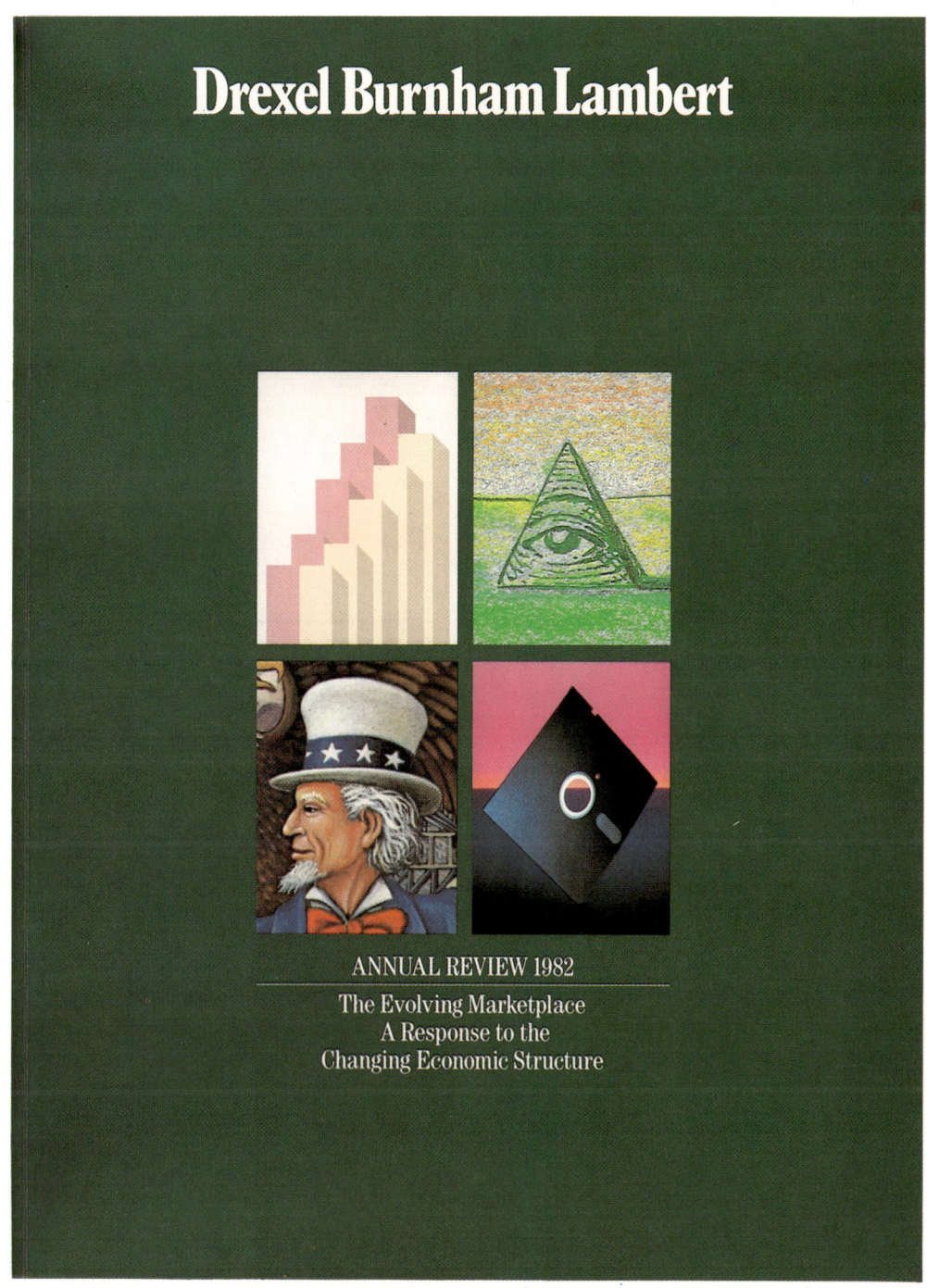

33/Annual Reports

were formed to reinforce this positioning."

The magazine format allows DBL to achieve this goal in a personal and informative way: by presenting a series of articles, some by-lined with names of DBL officers, on major financial issues (the role of the Federal Reserve, the effects of a mixed economy, the recent explosion of financial instruments, *et al*), DBL makes a strong case for the value of financial counseling, and by the way displays a good deal of its own knowledge and expertise. But, with four-color process, two PMS colors, and 100-pound Vintage Gloss text and cover papers, monthly magazines are seldom like this.

The articles are presented so that they communicate on several levels. First, they are themselves set in an up-sized reader face akin to the smaller one used in news magazines. Then, in case the reader does not find the text inviting enough or hasn't time to read it through, he or she can get the gist of the essay by reading a large-type, six-line summation that runs across the top of the essay's two-columned opening page. Finally, the articles are accompanied by photographs, illustrations, maps, and graphs—the usual stuffs of designed annual reports, here made unusual by virtue of their excellence: paintings by Eugene Mihaesco, Mark Hess, Richard Hess, Carol Donner, and Karl Hartig; and photos by Neil Selkirk and Ryszard Horowitz.

Following in the magazine vein, the financial section opens with a four-corner bleed photo of the accountant's letter, but here the resemblance to periodicals ends. The financial

statements have been printed on a gray-green background, with type and tables overprinted in black and forest green. This portion of the book, as well as the three-page "Resources and Major Activities" section that precedes it, is, of course, the technical heart of the report, and despite its conservative presentation, seems to have set the scale for the whole production.

The Pentagram Design group is itself worthy of a moment's attention. A relative newcomer to our shores, the British-based firm brings a fresh eye to the corporate reports it designs, as though its designers, having been raised in an atmosphere of benign socialism, have little awe and less fear of the established, "corporate" look. Their willingness to explore new forms, and their skill in making those forms work, suggests that substance can indeed be presented with no sacrifice of style.

Report: Drexel Burnham Lambert 1982. Investment research and financial services. Total 1982 assets $4.7 billion.
Design firm: Pentagram Design, New York City
Art director: Colin Forbes
Designer: Kaspar Schmid
Photographers: Neil Selkirk, Ryszard Horowitz
Illustrators: Eugene Mihaesco, Mark Hess, Richard Hess, Carol Donner and Karl Hartig
Copywriter: Colleen Sullivan
Printer: Case-Hoyt
Size: 9" by 12"; 48 pages plus covers
Quantity: 80,000

Management essays in a magazine format position this financial services group as a leader in the industry and an interpreter of trends.

35/Annual Reports

Digicon

The Digicon 1982 annual report is one of a rare breed: with an ultra-sensitivity to color, design, and production values, it fairly takes the breath away.

That this report succeeds to such a high degree is all the more surprising because, like the past four Digicon reports, it was conceived and developed with the efforts of three forces—the client, the advertising agency (Boswell Byers & Stone, Houston), and the design team (Gluth, Weaver, also of Houston).

"It's unusual, but it works well," account executive Don Boswell says about this three-way partnership. "The design firm works with the agency that works with the client. After five years, we all contribute. We collaborate, we work independently, then come together again. And it works because we're all seeking the same thing—impact, and the highest quality results."

And quality is what the 1982 Digicon report is about.

When the team met to discuss the report some five months before due-date, the problem was plainly put. Digicon had had another record year, with revenues of $163 million reflecting a 51 per cent increase over 1981 and 200 per cent over 1980. These superlative results had to be boldly displayed. But the client also wanted to visualize clearly its several areas of operations, and to explain a recent change in the structure of management of its major international business—geophysical data collection and processing.

To meet these objectives, the front of the book was divided into two sections—one for operations, one for

discussion of management reorganization. And while the two sections are discrete by virtue of content and organization, they are also stylistically linked by virtue of design.

First, these sections are rigorously divided into spreads—one per area of operation, one per management division. Furthermore, layout of each spread is governed by strict page formats: text/left, photo/right for operations but portrait and text/left, location photography/right for the management review.

Running through both sections like a grounding wire is a matte-finished black ink which forms the background for copy and graphs. The latter—brightly colored horizontal bars dropped into the black ground between blocks of banker's gray operations text—shine like gems on black velvet, reflecting the high colors of the photographs opposite. In the second section, the bands reappear in the form of an operations map, and the gray text is run on a narrow black band that separates the portrait from the location shot.

From the drama of a wrap-around cover landscape to the conservatively presented financial data, it is obvious that great care and planning went into the design and photography of this report. In the photo sections, every spread, by virtue of a carefully coordinated color palette, has its own mood, and yet that mood is restrained by the black text areas and half-inch, all-around white margins. Maintaining this control was especially tricky, Boswell tells us, in shooting the international section of the report. "The

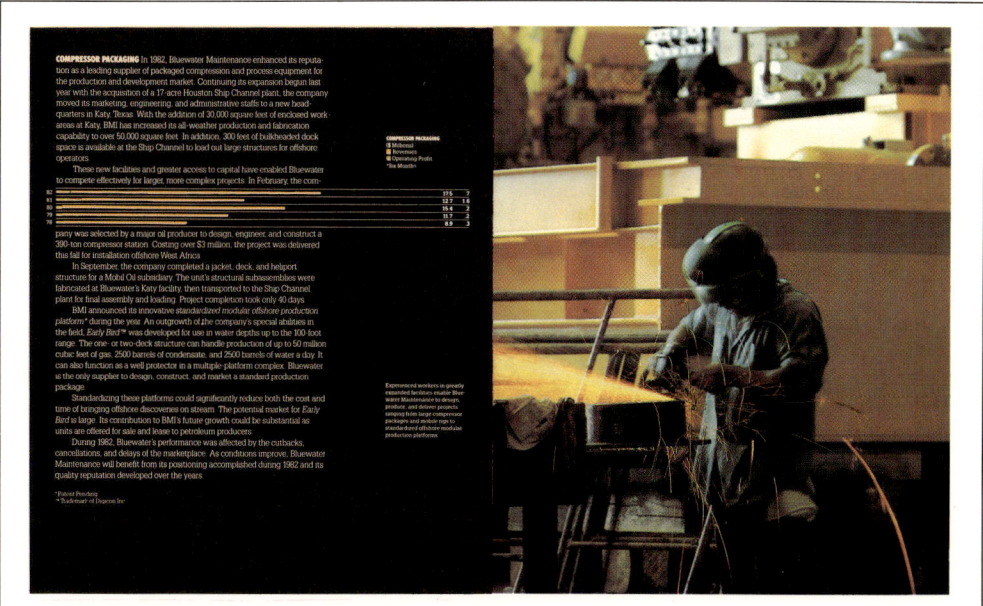

Produced by a three-way design team, report uses sensitive photography and simple graphs to tell an international marketing story.

37/Annual Reports

budget required using an unknown, local photographer in each area," he says. "Problems with lighting and backgrounds (the background color for each portrait is keyed to the location shot opposite) were handled by mail, or by international telephone calls interrupted by static."

Ultimately, however, all members of the design team were pleased. The glossy portions of the book were tucked between soft gray text divider pages; this sheet was also used to present financial information in the report's third and final section. The result is a colorful, innovative report that also means business.

"It's different," says Boswell in comparing this report with others designed by the same team. "But then it always is."

Report: Digicon, Inc. 1982. Geophysical, tug/supply, and compressor services to the gas and oil industry; seismic cable; computer peripherals; medical instruments. 1982 revenues $163 million.
Agency: Boswell Byers & Stone, Houston
Account executive: Don Boswell
Design firm: Gluth, Weaver, Houston
Art directors: John Weaver, Al Gluth
Designer: Al Gluth
Photographer: Bryan Smothers (major photography)
Copywriter: Judith Richards
Printer: George Rice & Sons
Size: 9" by 11"; 54 pages plus covers
Quantity: 27,000

Potlatch

Jonson Pedersen Hinrichs & Shakery has designed three consecutive annual reports for Potlatch Corporation, and all of these have been for business years that Potlatch's chairman and ceo, Richard B. Madden, has characterized as having tested the company's ability to cope.

Fiscal 1982—for which, the report shown here—had its particular difficulties. The longest and most severe decline in U.S. home-building since the Great Depression continued and, unlike other years, Potlatch's other forest-based businesses were unable to offset the housing recession's devastating effects.

Despite a decline in sales, Potlatch found encouragement in the success of certain management strategies, which permitted the company to maintain higher operating rates than for the paper industry as a whole. The company was also able to reduce its cash requirements, open new and improve old facilities, reduce salaried employment without layoffs, and divest itself of its sagging folding-carton operations. At the end of the third quarter of 1981, Potlatch was able to announce the holding of the common stock dividend to its current annual rate.

Proven performance of Potlatch management and a belief in the company's ability to hold its own in the future is at the root of the exuberance apparent in its 1982 report. Like many reports in this Casebook, it has a separate, visually overpowering theme section into which has been poured the lion's share of the report's focus and production, while the

operations review has been shrunk to a minimum number of pages.

The objective here, says Kit Hinrichs, the report's art director, "was to explore in depth one of Potlatch's major resources: the pine tree." To do so, he developed a 12-page section containing one spread devoted to each of six pine tree topics: varieties and distribution, history, growth, management, processing, and end use. Each spread is a lively montage of photographs, drawings, and copy blocks that comprise an encyclopedic attempt to reveal all that is important about pine.

Although Hinrichs had nine months to develop and produce the report and moved fairly quickly through storyboard and rough presentation stages, he found assembling the theme section to be demanding and time-consuming. While the concept called for a large quantity of original artwork, the budget didn't allow for it. So the designers were forced to rely on existing photography, archival materials from both Potlatch and the Forest Products Institute, and "found" art to supplement a modicum of assigned art and photography.

The result is a series of lively spreads that brightly contrast the serious, gray-toned format found in the rest of the book. All manner of elements have been assembled within the ruled borders of each spread (some even poke through them into the margins), and their varying shapes and sizes create a good deal of visual and textural interest. Furthermore, the approach allowed the designers a great deal of flexibility, as layouts could be easily adjusted

Tough times in the timber business have not prevented Potlatch from issuing another attractive and informative report.

Annual Reports/40

on a page-by-page, piece-by-piece basis.

The brief operations section that follows includes three pages of text, printed on a rich, warm gray and inset with full-color pictures representative of the various operating divisions. Headlines are dropped out, and page format is ruled all around with the same hairlines used in the theme section. Following are two pages of graphics—a facilities map and flow chart, much like that used in the 1981 report; from there the report moves smoothly and uninterruptedly into the financial review.

Typeface throughout the report—in keeping with the JPHS look for this client—is Times Roman in both roman and italic; paper is—what else?—the client's premium sheet, Quintessence Gloss, in cover and text weights.

Report: Potlatch Corporation 1982. Tree farming, wood converting, pulp and paper manufacturing. 1982 sales $820 million.
Design firm: Jonson Pedersen Hinrichs & Shakery, San Francisco
Art director: Kit Hinrichs
Designers: Kit Hinrichs, Barbara Vick
Photographers: Tom Tracy, Paul Fusco
Illustrators: Will Nelson, Justin Carroll
Copywriter: Delphine Hirasuna/Potlatch
Printer: Anderson Lithograph
Size: 8½" by 11"; 44 pages plus covers
Quantity: 65,000

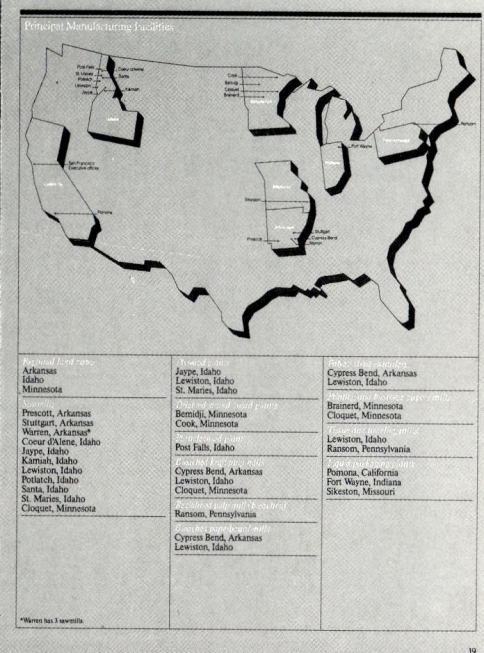

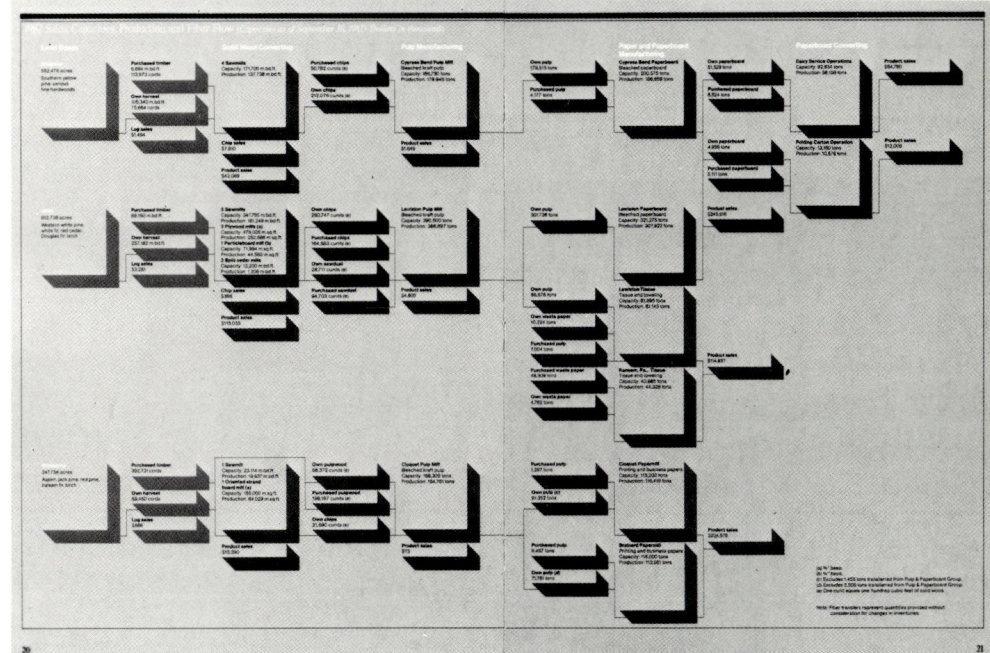

41/Annual Reports

Lomas & Nettleton Mortgage Investors

Reports produced by Richards, Sullivan, Brock for Lomas & Nettleton have been consistent winners in Casebook competitions. These two for Lomas & Nettleton Mortgage Investors (LNMI) continue a series reflecting the company's commitment to a particular quality of life and in themselves are variations on an even more focussed theme.

LNMI is in the business of making mortgage loans, principally for first mortgage construction and development. The 1981 LNMI report characterizes LNMI clients as among "the larger and more sophisticated real estate developers" who have been "moving increasingly toward the selective preservation of nature..." in their developments. These developers, according to Ron Sullivan, who art-directed and designed both of the reports shown here, "are developing with careful regard for the human needs which go beyond shelter. These builders have provided for or, in many cases, simply left intact natural 'green areas,' lakes, open space, and so on, to be used by those within the development."

To reflect this attitude of conscientious land use, Sullivan conceived two reports that would offer personal insights into these "green spaces" through pictographic representation and comments from the users themselves.

"We researched development in this country," says Sullivan about the 1981 report, "and found a number of sites illustrating this sort of 'responsible' development. We used photos of these sites, coupled with hand-written

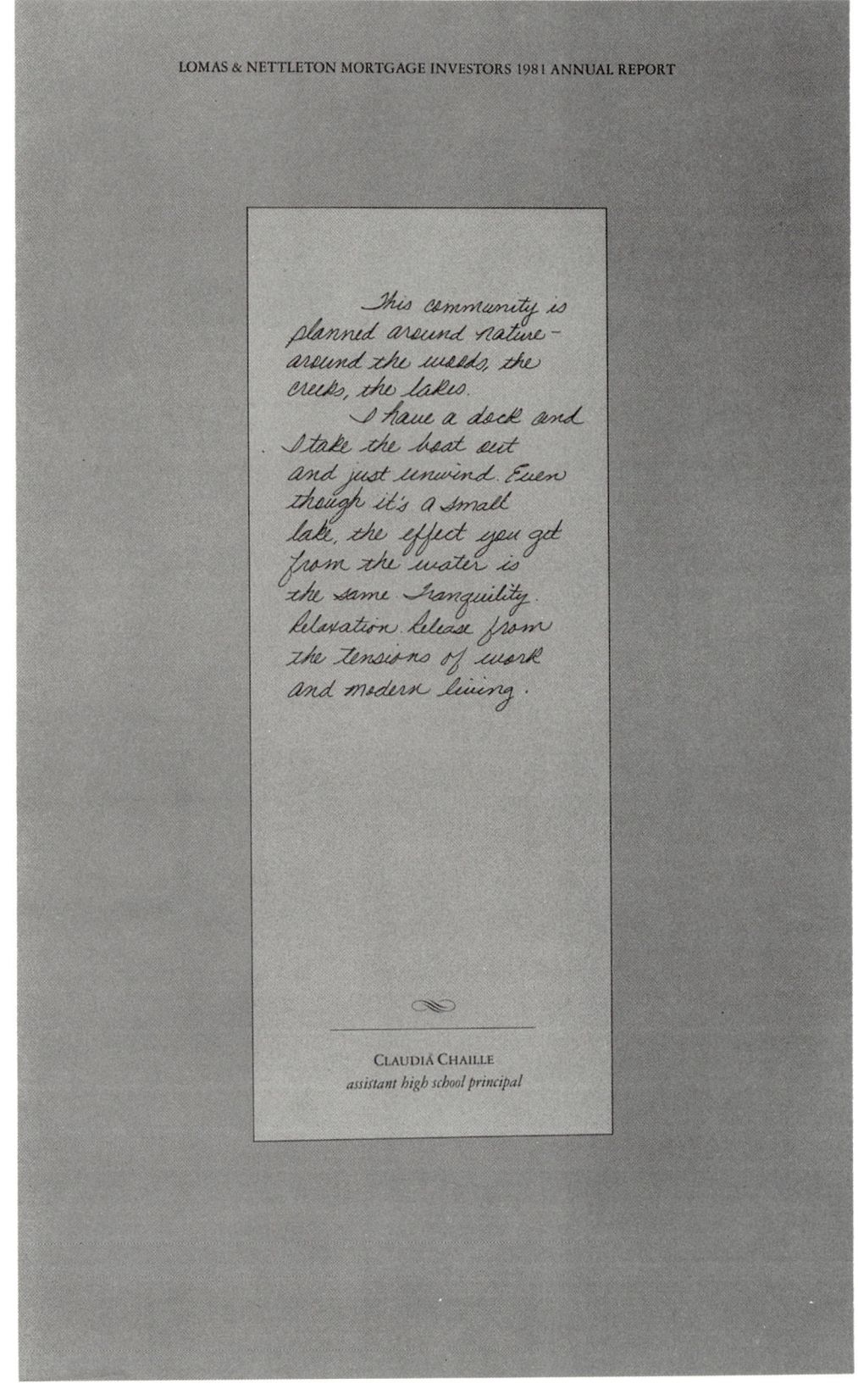

statements from individuals living in these areas, in an attempt to give full credibility to our purpose."

The basic format used for both the 1981 and 1982 reports is that used traditionally for LNMI. Narrower in size (7" by 11") than conventional reports, it calls for text set in one wide, single column per page; text spreads alternate with photo spreads. In the 1981 report, these photos cross the gutter and have caption-like quotations handwritten against a medium gray block to the right or left. Both photo and block are surrounded by a jet-black page.

Photos here are of a moody, misty sort—full-color with deep shadows and saturated colors. In one photo, the fog lifts off a suburban meadow; in another, the landscape is an all but indistinguishable backdrop to golden reflections from a private lake. The feeling here is not only one of respect for the land itself, but an awareness of the role the natural environment plays in the quality of human life.

In the 1982 LNMI report, the focus shifts from public open space to space that is more private. "Whereas the 1981 report concept concerned suburban development with green spaces for the development as a community," explains Sullivan, "the '82 report deals with urban development and smaller, garden-like areas for use by individuals as a retreat from the pressures of everyday urban life."

Following his usual mode of working, Sullivan and his staff searched for and located these private havens adjacent to or actually within individual urban

Two reports continue a series of "lifestyle" reports for a company in the business of making mortgage loans.

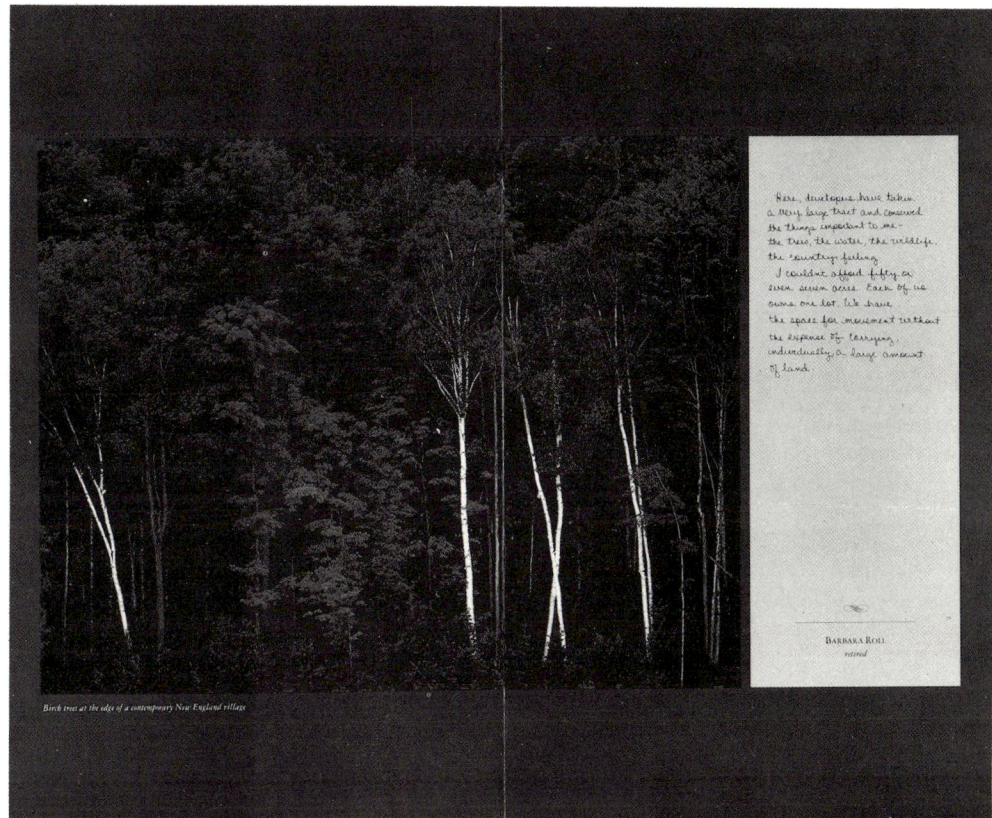

dwelling places. And, as in the previous report, he used quotes from individuals to express their importance in the lives of their users. Here, however, vertical photographs of similar muted tones are kept within the confines of a single narrow page. Presentation of user commentary takes its cue from a quote which appears on the report's covers. Eight lines from a poem by Andrew Marvell entitled "The Garden," this text begins in yellow-green and ends in a color akin to forest. Other quotes may start out in orange or brown or purply-blue, but all end on the same verdant note. (Although these blocks suggest the once more common split-fountain printing technique, they are actually rendered here in four-color process.)

Despite the smallness of the private spaces depicted, the report itself offers a good deal of open space. The individual photos are surrounded by white margins and come up against the gutter; the caption/quote sits at the far side of the page opposite, with nothing but white page all around. Below each, at the bottom margin, is a single, delicately tinted drawing of one or another garden flower. Text is set in the same face (Garamond) and to the same measure used in the previous reports, and a kraft-like flyleaf has been added to emphasize the introduction to and closing of the report.

In reviewing these two reports during the Casebook judging, one juror commented, "Real estate investment reports are usually full of houses or developments. But here's an innovative idea, and they're using it consistently. And the

**Mean while the Mind, from pleasures less,
Withdraws into it happiness:
The Mind, that Ocean where each kind
Does streight its own resemblance find;
Yet it creates, transcending these,
Far other Worlds, and other Seas;
Annihilating all that's made
To a green Thought in a green Shade.**

From Andrew Marvell's poem, 'The Garden'

idea is strong both in itself and in its context. It may be variations on a theme, but the designers are coming up with original variations."

For Ron Sullivan, who has designed eight LNMI reports, this has been his greatest challenge—"to consistently produce a book that is meaningful, provocative, and well-designed year after year."

"Looking out from our greenhouse, you see the tops of the trees and the clouds. Moving from a very dark duplex, it was exciting for us to have this space open to the sky. Indoors, there's the feel of nature, forever varied by changes in lighting from sunup to twilight and by the weather's shifts in mood."

Interior greenhouse in the residence of a young Dallas couple

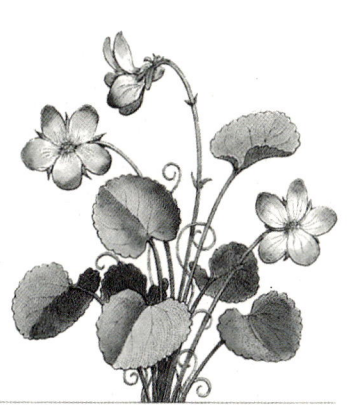

"I can go out on my balcony and feel removed from everything. I'll take a book and read for hours. I get so much pleasure having a space where I can grow flowers. I nurture the plants on the balcony, then rotate them around the house."

Balcony of a West Coast apartment

45/Annual Reports

"My garden is the way I create my own world and close the city behind me. And with the changing seasons, I can have many worlds. Mystery, too. I plant big plants in small spaces, partially hiding other plants, so you keep a sense of constantly coming upon new things."

Small garden at the rear of a row house in Washington, D.C.

Report: Lomas & Nettleton Mortgage Investors 1981 and 1982. Mortgage loan investment. 1981 revenues $44.6 million; 1982 revenues $39.9 million.
Design firm: Richards, Sullivan, Brock & Associates, Dallas
Art director/designer: Ron Sullivan
Photographer: Greg Booth
Illustrator: McRay Magleby (1982)
Copywriter: John Stone/Richards, Sullivan, Brock
Printer: Heritage Press
Size: 7" by 11"; 40 pages plus covers
Quantity: 20,000

LOMAS & NETTLETON MORTGAGE INVESTORS
STATEMENT OF SHAREHOLDERS' EQUITY

	Shares of Beneficial Interest	
	Number	Amount
Balance at July 1, 1979	3,700,000	$103,229,939
Net income		8,920,747
Dividends paid ($2.40 per share)		(8,880,000)
Balance at June 30, 1980	3,700,000	$103,270,686
Net income		10,231,108
Dividends paid ($2.62 per share)		(9,694,000)
Balance at June 30, 1981	3,700,000	$103,807,794
Net income		10,873,341
Dividends paid ($2.90 per share)		(10,730,000)
Balance at June 30, 1982	3,700,000	$103,951,135

See notes to financial statements

LOMAS & NETTLETON MORTGAGE INVESTORS
STATEMENT OF CHANGES IN FINANCIAL POSITION

	Year Ended June 30		
	1982	1981	1980
Cash at beginning of year	$ 16,478,562	$ 12,866,057	$ 14,138,038
Source of funds			
From operations:			
Net income	10,873,341	10,231,108	8,920,747
Payment of cash dividends	(10,730,000)	(9,694,000)	(8,880,000)
	143,341	537,108	40,747
Charges to allowance for possible losses	(3,086,293)	(1,399,341)	(1,101,174)
Deficiency of funds from operations after cash dividends	(2,942,952)	(862,233)	(1,060,427)
Collections on mortgage loans on real estate	228,238,968	357,538,037	363,414,430
Mortgage loans transferred to foreclosed properties	4,813,158	3,588,373	3,313,285
Cost of real estate sold	13,708,959	15,635,205	10,839,889
Decrease in long-term lease rentals receivable	19,848	258,416	27,320
Increase in short-term borrowings	17,558,627	—	—
Increase in accrued management fees	—	101,384	20,998
Increase in accrued interest and other liabilities	110,007	—	3,019,900
Increase in deferred income	888,003	653,550	—
Decrease in other assets	81,550	360,112	605,568
Total Funds Available after Cash Dividends	278,954,730	390,138,901	394,319,001
Applications of available funds			
Advances on mortgage loans on real estate	262,203,208	295,774,446	359,451,954
Additions to foreclosed properties	7,980,462	8,445,956	7,892,913
Increase in accrued interest and other receivables	1,205,078	181,650	958,883
Decrease in accrued management fees	48,908	—	—
Decrease in accrued interest and other liabilities	—	3,413,053	—
Decrease in deferred income	—	—	658,475
Decrease in short-term borrowings	—	63,345,234	9,990,719
Payments on long-term borrowings	2,500,000	2,500,000	2,500,000
Total Funds Applied	273,937,656	373,660,339	381,452,944
Cash at end of year	$ 5,017,074	$ 16,478,562	$ 12,866,057

See notes to financial statements

Annual Reports/46

Hospital Corporation of America

Hospital Corporation of America (HCA) management, in their letter to shareholders in the 1981 annual report, characterize that year as "the most significant year in HCA's corporate history." In 1981, the letter reports, the company established itself as a premier international health care company, with 349 hospitals owned or managed, for a total of 49,000 beds.

The underlying concept for HCA's 1981 report was to describe the various activities of a typical HCA international day. Conceived and executed by Bennett Robinson, with the assistance of Paula Zographos, both of Corporate Graphics in New York City, the book relies on strong documentary-style photography by Bruce Davidson to position HCA as a company capable of providing the highest standards of health care, both effectively and profitably.

This photo essay, which comprises 14 pages of the "designed" portion of the report, is preceded by a goals and policy statement and a page of introductory copy. Here, the designers make good use of the advantages provided by perfect binding to easily mix papers. While the photo section is printed on 100-pound Cameo dull uncoated stock, these two leaves and the financial section are of Curtis Tweedweave in a pale gray; this text stock is also used in a darker shade and heavier weight for the report's cover.

In addition, the book opens and closes with the Cameo sheet—a single leaf has been tipped inside the front cover (the missing leaf from that 14-page photo essay signature), and an additional eight-page

form at the back presents corporate information, including a photograph of HCA's corporate headquarters in Nashville, Tennessee. There is no separate section comprising an operations review—this text has been folded into the financial report.

This adds up to a fairly straightforward solution, and it might have gone by the board in the Casebook judging were it not for a design device that provides a unifying motif and just the right finishing touch. Running through the front portion of the report is a broad horizontal band composed of many vertical lines. Below this "time-line" are hung captions describing the activities pictured. The HCA day begins at 12 noon in Nashville, where the time-line is printed in sunny yellow, and proceeds through the color spectrum as the essay moves around the world, returning to Nashville—and sunny yellow—once more. Between hues of violet and blue—the turning point in the color spectrum and midnight in the HCA "day"—the time-line turns black; on the cover, where the motif begins and is technically not a time-line at all, it appears in white; and it changes to pale gray on the leaf bearing highlights and executive portraits.

One would suppose that the easiest way to print this line-through-the-rainbow would be through some sort of split-font arrangement, but this obviously wasn't possible, since the object being printed was not a single flat image but a 16-page form. Thus, the time-line was screened and printed with process colors (with a gloss black added for the "midnight"

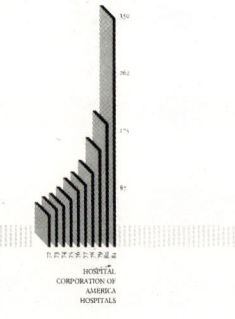

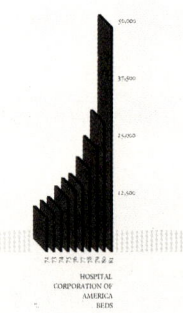

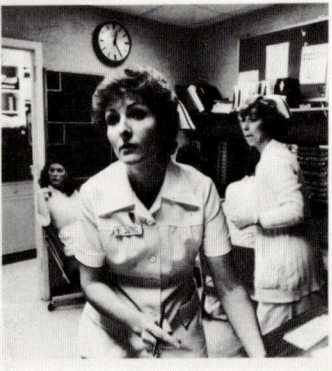

portion), making tight registration important. "Achieving a gradual color development was difficult," comments Robinson.

We don't wonder that it was.

Report: Hospital Corporation of America 1981. Health care through hospital ownership and management. 1981 revenues $2.4 billion.
Design firm: Corporate Graphics, New York City
Art director: Bennett Robinson
Designers: Bennett Robinson, Paula Zographos
Photographer: Bruce Davidson
Copywriter: Vic Campbell
Printer: The Hennegan Co.
Size: 8½" by 11½"; 58 pages plus covers
Quantity: 70,000

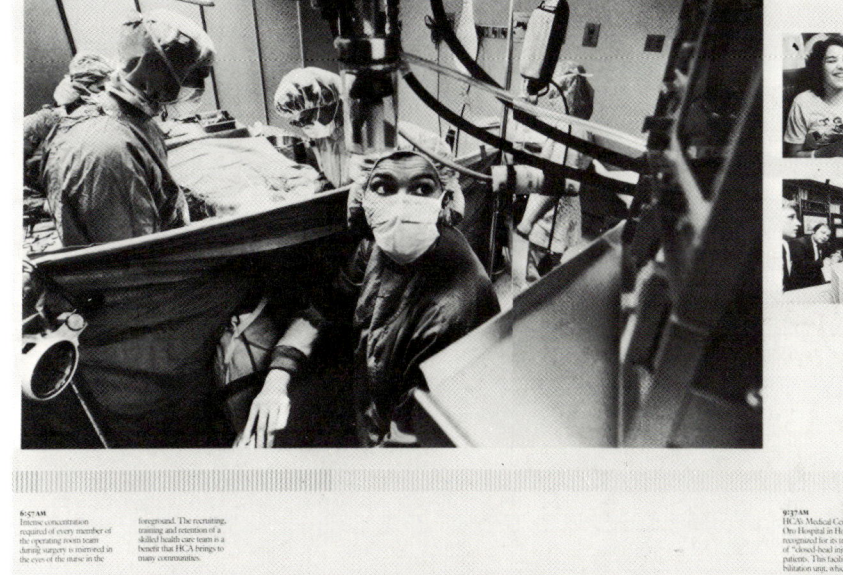

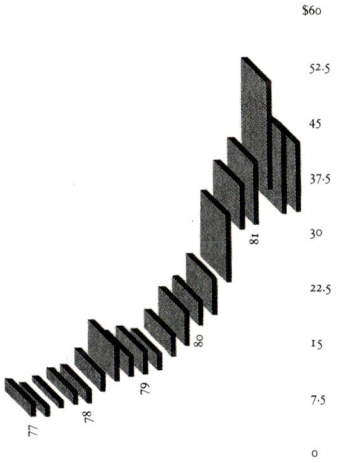

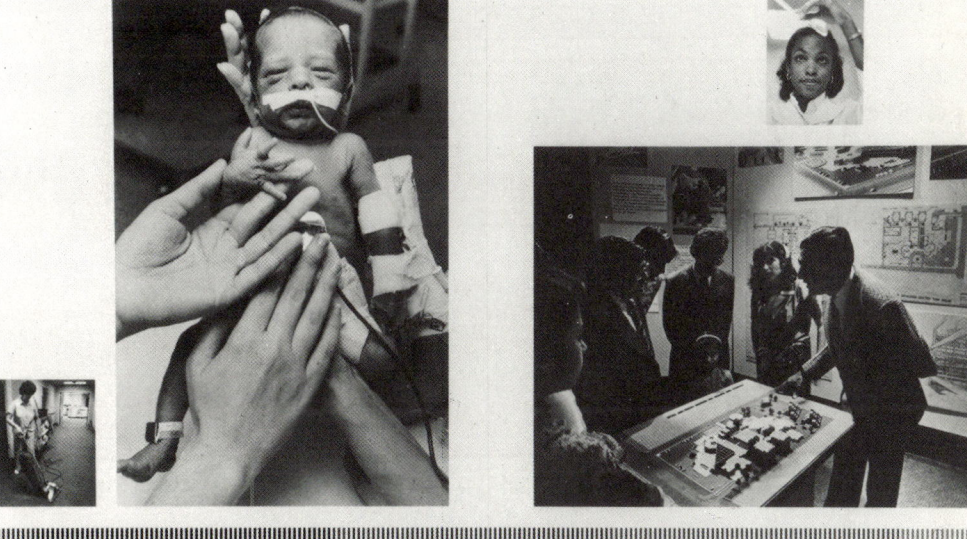

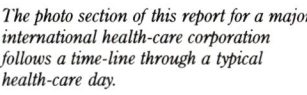

The photo section of this report for a major international health-care corporation follows a time-line through a typical health-care day.

49/**Annual Reports**

Save the Children

"This is a nitty-gritty little book that, because of its small format, doesn't play games," said one Casebook juror about the 1981 Save the Children report. His point was well taken. With little more than $20,000 to spend on 10,000 copies, designers Tom Morin and Henry Goerke at Jack Hough Associates (JHA) had to make every penny count.

Save the Children—a nonprofit agency well-known for its services to children and its community self-help assistance—had several goals in mind for this report. In addition to describing the ways in which its funds had been used to serve children, the client wanted to report on the progress it had made in effecting community-wide change, thereby improving the total environment of children around the globe. The organization was also entering its 50th anniversary year and wanted to make some special presentation in recognition of that fact.

JHA principal Jack Hough met with Save the Children president David L. Guyer and his director of public relations, Elizabeth Woodward, to discuss these objectives and plan the report. Since Save the Children had existing photographs of children and programs and no money for assigned photography, it was imperative that these images be used. Fortunately, comments Goerke, although most of these lacked the quality and consistency of good annual report photography, "they were refreshingly honest and spontaneous."

In initial meetings, it was decided to work within the

agency's traditional 6" by 9" format to create a report which would organize and communicate its relatively complex story both clearly and simply; the photographs would be augmented with artwork by children from the communities served. The hope was that the combination of elements would evoke a sense of the rich and varied cultures served by Save the Children, as well as project a feeling for its lively, people-oriented activities.

After concept approval, the next step was to "assign" the children's art. Reports Goerke: "We put out a call to children in various countries for drawings and paintings to include in the report, and also sent along art materials and instructions so that their work could be reproduced. Not unlike the professional artists we sometimes use, the children disregarded our instructions but did a great job anyway."

In an effort to make the budget appear larger than it really was, the designers developed the report with printing forms and imposition in mind, and ended up using only one eight-page four-color form—with no four-color separations. The remaining three forms were printed in two colors—black with a different matched color for each. They also spent time counting and adjusting the number of photos, illustrations, and screens for each page so as to curtail expenses.

The cover of the book features a single graphic—a large "1981" made up of images symbolizing Save the Children's worldwide involvement for the past 50 years. Inside, pages are

A low-budget report for a non-profit organization presents a lively picture of services to children around the world.

Left: Hearts hung on the Valentine Tree symbolize concern for children around the world.
Right: Village life in Mexico.

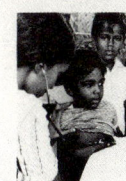

Below: Children are examined in a Sri Lankan nutrition clinic.
Left: A child's home in Tunisia.
Right: Farming the fields of Nepal.

51/Annual Reports

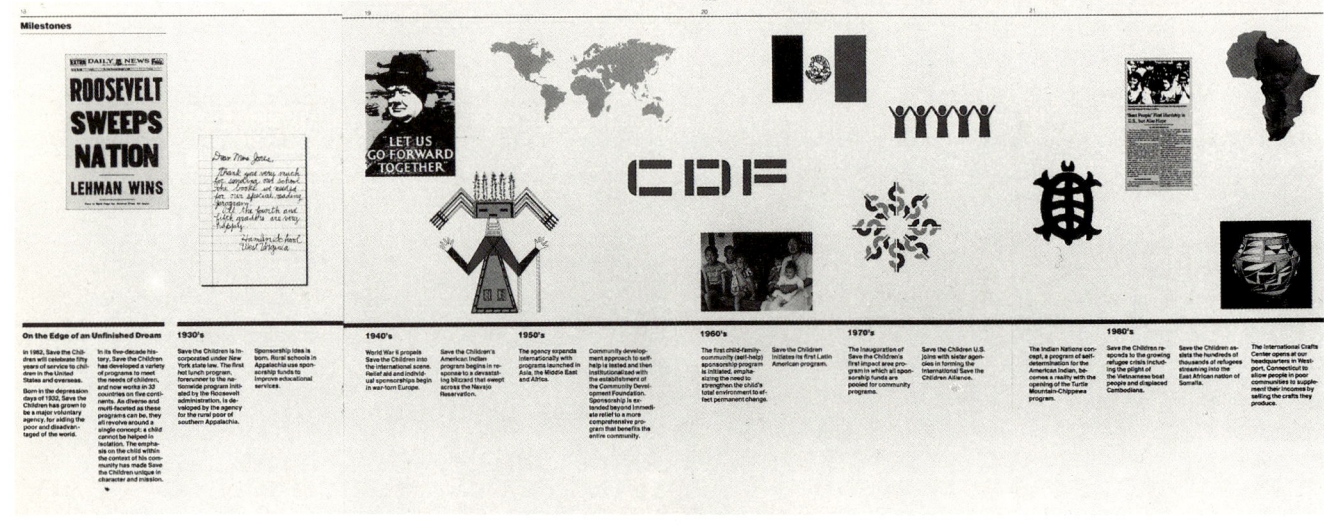

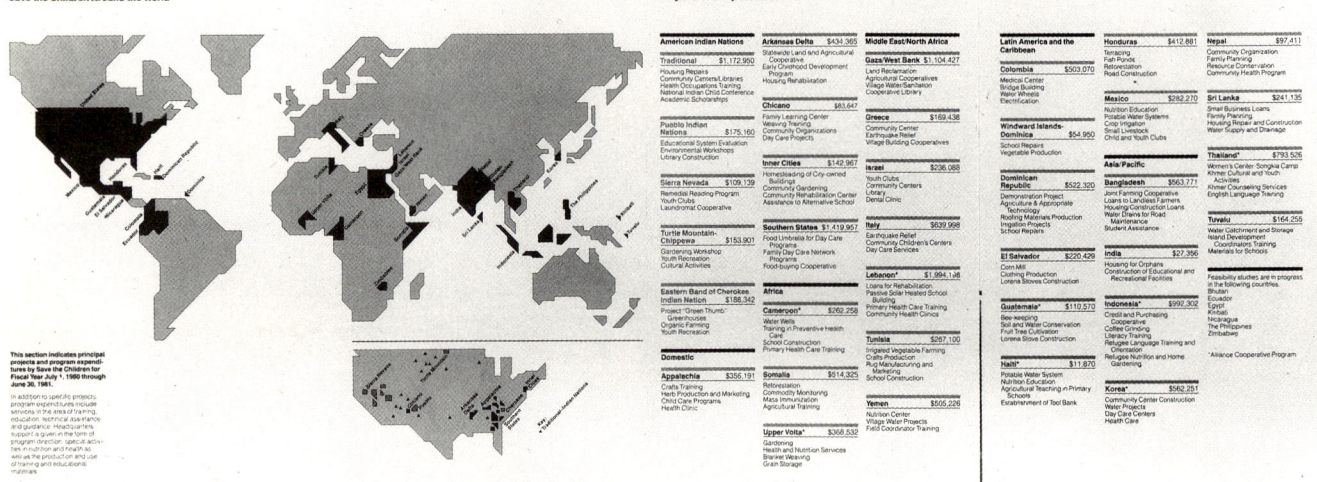

divided horizontally to allow for running text above and photos/artwork below. While reportage is in two columns per page, other reference information is presented in a three-column format. Helvetica in three weights is used throughout.

To celebrate the anniversary, the designers developed a timeline across a six-page fold-out, on one side featuring, through "found" artwork, milestones in the agency's history, on the other, a world map. Depicting locations where Save the Children is in service, the map is color-keyed to a detailed listing of projects and expenditures which immediately follows.

For a design firm which produces some two dozen corporate annual reports each year, designing a report for an organization like Save the Children was somewhat unusual. For Henry Goerke, it was "a nice change of pace to do an annual report where children are the center of attention."

Report: Save the Children 1981. Non-profit agency serving children and sponsoring community self-help. 1981 total revenues $19.8 million.
Design firm: Jack Hough Associates, Stamford, CT
Art director: Tom Morin
Designer: Henry Goerke
Copywriter: Hank Snelling
Printer: Eastern Press
Size: 6" by 9"; 36 pages plus covers
Quantity: 10,000

Thermo Electron

As a pioneer in developing ways to use energy more efficiently, Thermo Electron is a company closely followed by the financial community. Its management are scientists and theoreticians among the tops in their fields, and, as pressures in the oil and energy markets have increased, they have continually seemed to exist on the brink of a discovery. And it was just this view of the company that the 1981 Thermo Electron annual report was conceived to reinforce.

In developing that concept, designers Mike Weymouth and Tom Laidlaw dealt directly with the company's corporate communications editor, Ann Barrett, and its president, George Hatsopoulos. "Very few corporate executives approach their report with as much interest as George Hatsopoulos," says Weymouth. "To him, the annual is not merely a report of what has been accomplished, but an opportunity to address the great energy issues that we as a nation confront."

To achieve these goals, the book was organized into several sections which would offer greater interest than a more typically organized report. Following company convention, the cover, here printed in shades of gray on white, consisted of a graphic, diagrammatic treatment—in this case, a simplified version of a more complicated diagram appearing inside.

Following a highlights page made up entirely of gray-on-gray bar graphs, the designers developed a two-page spread meant to provide an overview of the company: on the left, an explanatory text, and on the right, a glossy sheet stacked

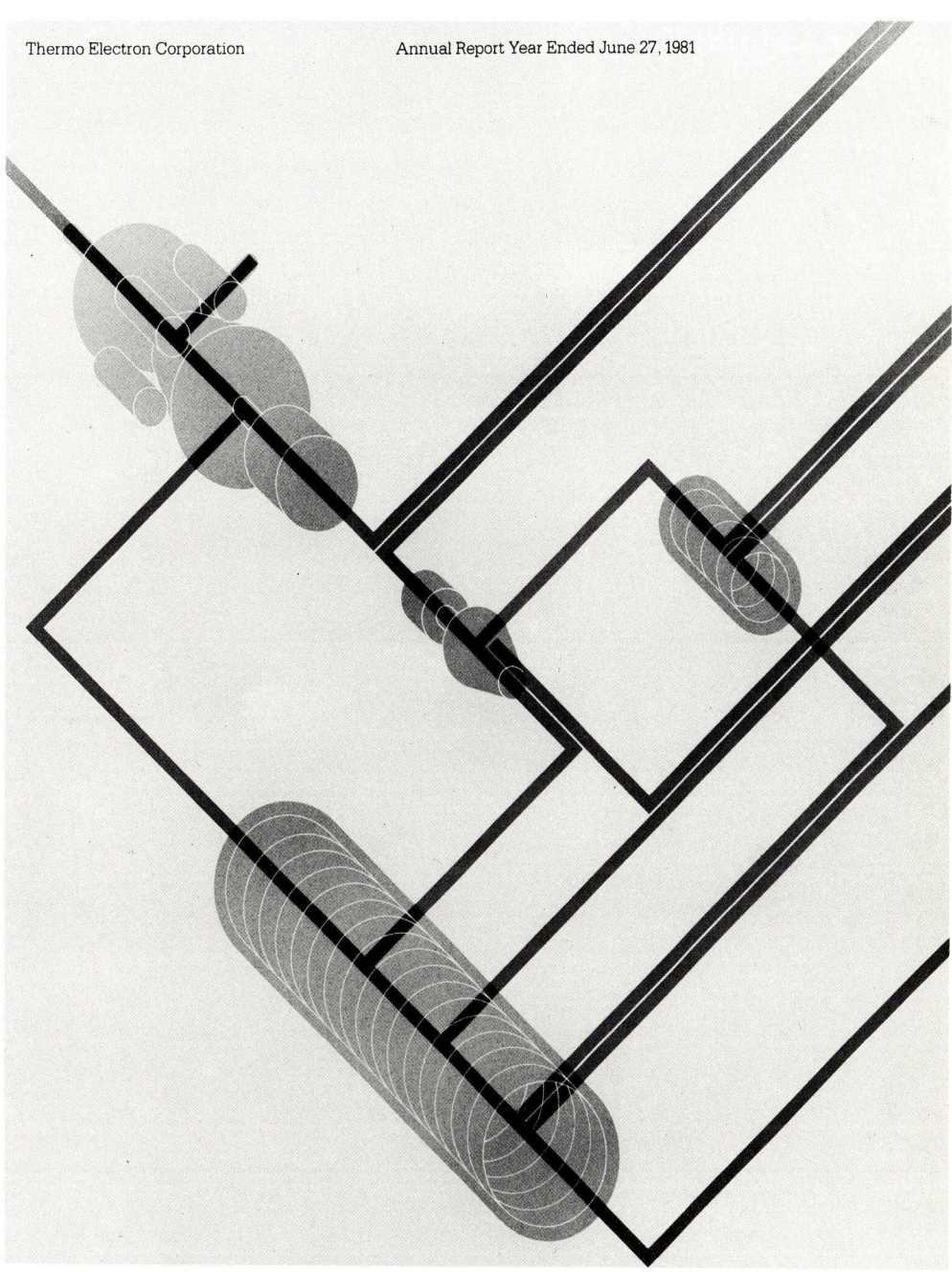

Thermo Electron Corporation   Annual Report Year Ended June 27, 1981

53/Annual Reports

with four narrow horizontal photographs, bleeding all around. "We felt it was important here and throughout the book," notes Weymouth, "to convey quickly that the company has many tangible product lines—as well as a grasp on where the energy problem is taking the country." The photos, therefore, are close-up and cropped tightly, offering the reader a look inside the workings of Thermo Electron.

The operations section of the book is really two sections. The first, a question-and-answer treatment, offers management a chance to talk about the company while revealing some of their management expertise. The second section, entitled "Energy Outlook," is an essay focussing on various problems and possibilities within the energy industry. Both sections are enhanced through photography, diagrams, charts, and extended captions.

"If I had to give one reason for this report's appeal," says Weymouth, "it would have to be that it not only contains a wealth of information, but projects its image through the use of design elements. It suggests *visually* that the information is there, that one doesn't have to struggle through the text to gain insight into the company."

A note on production. This report, like a few others in this Casebook, uses a double saddle-wire binding to mix papers and cluster production effects. Operations sections, printed in four-color process plus two PMS colors, is on Quintessence Gloss, while financials (a leaf of which wraps around the repro sheet) are in

Annual Reports/54

two colors on Kilmory gray. The complexity of the production is part and parcel with the complicated, "designed" look of the report.

And yet this look is not design for design's sake. "This is the first and only report we've done for Thermo Electron," says Weymouth. "Their past reports had often been singled out by some of the major design competitions, so the switch certainly wasn't to upgrade the design. I feel that we fulfilled the goal of making these 'design tricks' an integral part of the overall statement."

Since the design of this report, Thermo Electron has installed an in-house art department to do, among other things, its annual report—"a move," comments Weymouth, "that seems natural for a company whose bread-and-butter is efficiency."

Report: Thermo Electron Corporation 1981. Process equipment, co-generation power systems, monitoring instruments, and manufacturing services for industry. 1981 net sales and revenues $210 million.
Design firm: Weymouth Design, Boston
Art director: Michael Weymouth
Designer: Thomas Laidlaw
Photographers: Michael Weymouth, Larry Long
Copywriter: Thermo Electron
Printer: Acme Printing
Size: 8½" by 11"; 40 pages plus covers
Quantity: 10,000

A company involved in energy research and technology uses its annual report to address the great energy issues confronting the nation.

55/Annual Reports

Warner
Communications

It has been said before in these Casebook pages that Warner Communications, Inc. (WCI) is a company for whom entertainment is big business. In 1982, the company's earnings once again reached record levels, with earnings per share up 11 per cent and revenues just under $4 billion.

And it has also been said here that Warner is a company that puts all of its corporate promotion dollars into its annual report. Five of WCI's previous reports—all by the same design firm—have been selected by Casebook jurors; this, the 1982 report, is the third designed since by another firm, Pentagram, and shows every evidence of keeping up Warner's high standards of style.

In fact, there are several traits immediately linking it to its predecessors. One is the use of a rich Payne's gray for the cover color—a WCI tradition as long as most people can remember. Another is that the WCI report, like the company itself, is big: this one measures 9½" by 11" and packs 102 pages inside its covers, only 26 of which are about financial reporting. The book also utilizes a Garamond typeface, premium papers and lush photography.

It seems, then, that what distinguishes the 1982 WCI report is not so much a matter of difference, but of degree. Judging by the company's annuals, especially those since 1977, WCI has been steadily moving away from an image of flash and dash to one of a serious business that happens to market entertaining products. It has managed to position what once might have been considered frivolous as desirable, even necessary, and has made money at it.

In the report at hand, we find the most restrained, least glamorous WCI to date. There are no spotlighted stars, no generic still-lifes linking up movie stills, sports shots, and photos of cosmetics and electronic games. The focus here is marketing—and international marketing, at that.

"The special problem of this report," says Pentagram's Peter Harrison, its art director, "was to portray WCI as having markets outside the continental U.S.A." Because of this goal, the famous faces and memorable scenes are downplayed; in fact, in the whole of the operations review, they don't appear at all.

Instead, Harrison has taken the report, turned it into a horizontal format, and divided it into discrete sections—five of them—of which, from a design standpoint, the review of operations and a special photo section are the most interesting.

Whereas in former years the WCI operations review was the place for any splash and dazzle, this year's review is surprisingly low-key. A simple running text fills the center four columns of each six-column spread, with the outer columns being used for rather funky little illustrations that point up various parts of the text. Here and there a gray-backgrounded bar chart, which reverses from a pale gray grid underlying the illustrations, replaces one of the spots.

This graph paper-like grid, introduced on the cover of the report as the basis for a

stylized global map, continues as somewhat of a leitmotif for the whole book. It reappears, again reversed, in small bar graphs running along a highlights fold-out on page one, as graphs in management's policy statements, and again as the cover design, scaled down, to introduce the eye-grabbing photo section following the operations review.

Clearly, we have arrived at the *sine qua non* of this report: large, lush horizontal photographs run full-page or perhaps spill across the gutter; smaller, cameo shots support the larger image as well as the accompanying text.

And accompanying text is what this is. If most annual reports use photographs to pull a reader into the copy, this one seems to make photography the major medium; in this section at least, text becomes an informal, readable soft-sell that ties together particular images with the presence of one or another WCI product in use worldwide.

But, again, it is the photography that is truly riveting and, in a few cases, somehow disturbing. If we like the looks of an English country gentleman bringing home an Atari computer, or Parisian street musicians interpreting a song by Warner artist Jackson Browne, what are we to make of Donna Sommers singing her heart out, via battery-powered record player, to a group of Masai tribesman? Or a Buddhist monk in Thailand who watches a televised Kung Fu series while keeping his evening temple vigil? The report makes its point. We are ever more increasingly members of a "global village";

57/Annual Reports

still, one can't help but wonder if something isn't being lost.

Whatever this report's emotional appeal, the designers were able to achieve their objectives. By using one major photographer and one illustrator, a graphic consistency has been maintained that was at times lacking, albeit not deleteriously, in previous reports, and they were able to keep within the budget of those years. "By using one photographer and no expensive styling or models or sets," says Harrison, "location photography actually proved less expensive."

A report for the entertainment giant avoids flash and dazzle for the business of international marketing.

Report: Warner Communications, Inc. 1982. Music recording and publishing; filmed, theater, and sports entertainments; direct-response marketing; publishing; cable communications; cosmetics. 1982 revenues $3.98 billion.
Design firm: Pentagram Design, New York City
Art director: Peter Harrison
Designer: Susan Hochbaum
Photographers: Phillip Jones Griffiths (major photography), Arnold Newman, Peter Harrison
Illustrator: Kip Lott
Copywriter: David Bither/WCI
Printer: Case-Hoyt
Size: 9½" by 11"; 102 pages plus covers
Quantity: 150,000

Annual Reports/58

Knudsen

"This is a beautiful annual report," said one Casebook juror about the Knudsen Corporation 1981 annual report, "especially when you think of all the things it could have been—warehouses, trucks, a family sitting in the kitchen eating their products. And this is so simple—it says everything the other kind of annual report would have said, but it says it better and easier."

Knudsen is a dominant producer of dairy products in the state of California, with increasing penetration into out-of-state markets. It enjoys a strong consumer image as a brand of uncompromising, consistent quality, and several of its products hold leading market shares.

The company's 1981 report reflects this position of leadership and quality through an unusual design approach that avoids all of the clichés of most food reports. And by bringing to the task a sensitive eye, designer Rik Besser, of Robert Miles Runyan & Associates, has created a report that is more about feeling than format—and that sets new standards for food reports.

The dominant force here, as in most contemporary reports, is color photography, but it is photography of an uncanny elegance. Beginning with twin shots of Knudsen ice cream products on the report's covers and ranging through the report on operations, the photos present single portions of Knudsen products arranged as if for serving. Great care has been taken as to colors and position of serving pieces—plates, spoons, glassware—and the jewel-like still-lifes, with their gleaming dinnerware,

Knudsen Corporation

1981 Annual Report

precisely placed garnishes, and overhead camera angle are reminiscent of the artfully arranged and elegantly presented food served in fine Japanese restaurants.

"We wanted to show Knudsen's products in a new and interesting fashion," says Besser, "to give the book a simple but strong graphic look, while maintaining a degree of richness and elegance."

Besser achieved these goals by orchestrating the report's other design elements so as to harmonize with the mood established by the photographs. He selected a premium grade gloss sheet for use throughout the report, then printed a tint of yellow across cover, photograph, and financial pages. Headlines, simple horizontal bar graphs, and the book's only graphic ornament—bold vertical bars that reach into text pages at the upper left margin and mark off caption areas at the bottom—are printed a rich reddish-brown. On the photo spreads, headline color remains consistent, while color bars are printed variously to reflect the background color in the photograph opposite.

Touches to text and type—in addition to the color headlines—include the spelling out of page numbers ("one, two," etc.) and the use throughout the book of one typeface—Palatino Italic. "I feel that serif italics look more personal and hand-written," Besser comments, "and Palatino doesn't get too 'scripty'- looking."

By such careful consideration, the designer has managed to convey the expressed feeling of "making the images 'art' and maintaining

a simple and harmonious balance with all of the elements." And, for his client's sake, he has at the same time turned simple foodstuffs into items of character and dignity. As one juror put it, "This report makes cottage cheese look important." And for a producer of dairy products, that says it.

Exquisite product still-lifes light up a report for a producer of dairy and related foods.

Report: Knudsen Corporation 1981. Dairy and related food products; flavorings; agricultural management; deli/grocery stores. 1981 revenues $464 million.
Design firm: Robert Miles Runyan & Associates, Los Angeles
Art director: Robert Miles Runyan
Designer: Rik Besser
Photographer: Robert Stevens
Copywriter: Knudsen Corp.
Printer: Lithographix
Size: 8½" by 11"; 32 pages plus covers
Quantity: 20,000

61/Annual Reports

H. J. Heinz

H.J. Heinz enjoys an enviable position among food processors. As one of the world's largest food businesses, it employs some 45,000 people in 100 administrative and production facilities worldwide, and its name and keystone label are globally known. Moreover, it has enjoyed a steady growth in profits during the past ten years, during general hard times as well as during ups and downs specific to the food industry.

Yet, despite its reputation as a healthy food giant, or perhaps because of it, Heinz has in its annual reports endeavored to shape its image in human terms. By creating through its employees a feeling of trust, warmth, and friendliness, the company has downplayed its scope and diversity and subtly stressed its involvement in food, that most basic and most necessary of human commodities.

Since 1977, these people-oriented reports have been designed by Corporate Graphics, and one or more of them have appeared in each Annual Report Casebook. The books as a whole have been continuously well-designed, to be sure, and yet they are not of a piece by any means. Far from being variations on a theme, these books are more like explorations of humanness, and in sequence their conclusions have been increasingly refined.

Past expressions of Heinz's people theme have included sensitively written accounts of certain employees in their off-hours or personal statements about their individual problems, feelings, and concerns. Others have presented broader contexts—harvest time around

The world is never the same once a good poem has been added to it.—Dylan Thomas

Heinz This H.J. Heinz Company Annual Report for 1982 contains more than the usual corporate accounting of a 12-month fiscal period. The year speaks for itself, and a good year it was, for the company and for its shareholders. The proof has been detailed between these covers. It need not be repeated here. ■ Let us talk instead about some remarkable people. ■ First, ten Heinz employees, who responded notably well when challenged to express themselves by way of poetry. ■ Then, ten of the world's leading illustrators, who applied skill and imagination to enhance what those employees had written. ■ Their story is inside.

the world, or processing and enjoying that harvest. One report was like a huge yearbook—a once-and-for-all documentation of the extended Heinz family, bound separately from and slip-cased with the financial portion of the report. Each report has been individually conceived by Heinz management and designed by Corporate Graphics with a fresh eye.

The obvious difference in the design of the 1982 Heinz report is its departure from photographic reportage. Whereas previous reports in the series have relied on photos to create the desired visual impression, this report uses illustration. And the illustrations in themselves are not literal portraits of people or even aspects of Heinz, but evocative paintings meant to expand the accompanying text—poems by ten Heinz employees.

Truly, this is a report to be read. For as photographs are to the more literal meanings of prose, paintings are to the emotionally charged imagery of poetry. If past Heinz reports have revealed its employees' politics and private passions, this one probes even more deeply into their psyches.

To find the poems, Heinz management sponsored a poetry contest. More than 700 entries were received from 300 employees, and from those

UNTITLED

The sun shines above the horizon,
Orange and yellow in hue.
The wind shimmers the trees,
Wafting unaware leaves
              to the ground,
Unmindful of our love
Where it is also bound
Amid the dying others.

Carol Whitmore, data entry clerk, Heinz U.S.A.

THE SUGAR CANE FIELD
(Puerto Rico)

The flirting of sugar cane tops
with the undulating winds
Jungle entangled with climbing
itching vines
Burning fire enclosured INFERNO;
Concerto of roaring machetes;
Sugar Cane field
that swallows our JIBARO
Dying in the unconquerable
jungle;
Water boy;
Water boy;
Shout our JIBARO
Oh, GOD I'm burning

In the farness
the Sugar Mill
depicting the sky
with vomiting dark
smokes
Polluted balsams
that shortened our
lives;

The sun sets over the horizon
Retreat for our JIBARO
Oh, everlasting struggle;
The Man and the Sugar Cane Field;
Tomorrow;
The reward
A small bag of corn meal, black coffee
& trade mark "COLLINS" MACHETE

Day breaks, again
Brandishing & trembling Machetes;
Burning bodies
Imprisoned Souls;
Cruel destiny embalmed with sweats
in the Sugar Cane Field
Struggles ceased
Returning home
Face down, glancing over our
Mother Earth;
TOMORROW;
The same;
"JIBARO"
Till death
Knock on your door;
Cruel World;;

Milton Rosado, plant superintendent, Star-Kist Caribe, Puerto Rico

A major food producer finds personal expression in employee poetry and professional illustration.

63/Annual Reports

were selected the ten poems in the report. None of the "poets" had been published before, and all spoke of people and events that had somehow affected their lives.

The winning poems were sent to ten of the world's top illustrators. After discussions with art director Bennett Robinson, the artists executed and submitted final artwork—no sketches or roughs were made for approval beforehand.

The poems and paintings were organized into a discrete section forming the heart (or perhaps soul) of the report. The only disappointing aspect here is that, while the Heinz poets are immediately identified, those ten top illustrators are not. So it is by their signatures or styles that we know who they are at this point. However, this oversight is remedied for those who read on: the spread immediately following the poems contains comments from both poets and artists, in the first case speaking of poetry and poetry writing, and in the second, speaking of a personal response to a particular poem. It's unusual enough to find employees speaking for and about themselves in an annual report; to find artists like James McMullan, Robert Weaver, Paul Davis, and Jean-Michel Folon commenting on their assignments in a corporate document is truly extraordinary.

KENNEDY AIRPORT: MIDNIGHT

Chrome-encrusted bird of prey
Swoops him up a world from me.
I wave at windows blurred as darkened O-shape
    Cartoon mouths
        Agape without a cry.
In skeletal aloneness now
I make my midnight way
Through parking lots barren of humankind
As though each soul were vanished/banished
/Quite computerized:
"ARRIVALS"
    (At what new-found ports of pain?)
"DEPARTURES"
    (From fields forfeit of hope)
"CARRYING A DANGEROUS WEAPON?"
    Yes.
    (It's called "regret"...and self-destructs.)
Not every jet-streaked death falls screaming from the skies.
Some in shrouded silence come.
"EXIT" command the signs
And "TERMINAL"—a label pinned on love.

Anne Hosansky, manager-editorial services, Weight Watchers International

AUGUST

A fugue
of two white chairs
in an off-white room.

Touch
the reoccurring theme
Feel
the related melodies
Hold
the dissonant harmony.

All come
together
in the
counterpoint
of a
summer's night.

Edna Schneider, lecturer, Weight Watchers International

Annual Reports/64

As spectacular as this section seems, it is well balanced by the other parts of the report. The book opens with highlights and the shareholders' letter, printed in brown on an ivory text sheet that is also used in the closing financials. Between the letter and poetry section is sandwiched the operations report proper, and here we see the designers' art at its subtle best. Text is set into wide columns that fill two-thirds of the page—a grid that, when extended into other sections, allows poems to be positioned with care and financial tables and notes to be read with ease. Into the remaining third of the page are set spot illustrations by the same artists, marking off various areas of operations.

An interesting organizing factor in the report's opening sections is the use of hollow and solid squares. These little devices are usually more appealing to editors than to designers, but in this case, they work. In the letter, each solid brown square introduces a new paragraph; in the operations review, where each paragraph is really a short take on one of Heinz's diverse businesses, the squares are outlined in black and filled with a gentle ochre.

Report: H.J. Heinz Company 1982. Food and food processing. 1982 sales $3.7 billion.
Design firm: Corporate Graphics, New York City
Art director: Bennett Robinson
Designers: Bennett Robinson, Paula Zographos
Illustrators: Robert Weaver, Paul Davis, David Wilcox, Carolyn Brady, Edward Sorel, John Collier, Jean-Michel Folon, Robert M. Cunningham, Robert Giusti, James McMullan
Copywriter: Oscar Shefler
Printer: George Rice & Sons
Size: 8½" by 11"; 70 pages plus covers
Quantity: 50,000

RIVERING

A Venetian groan
rouses the rivers
from a shrouded dawn....

Mirages of barges
slide past pilasters
and
unhazed and abrupt
from the spectral murk
of a thousand bridges
appear.

In unstartling profile
they addle
the fist-rubbing eye
of the morning
and move it to
vulnerable love
as
link upon link
of the stuff of the nation
silently glide
in head-lowered hush
for the humble
and beautiful might
of this Venice
of ours.

65/Annual Reports

Lockheed

Since its well-publicized financial difficulties some years ago, Lockheed Corporation has been watched with interest from various financial quarters. But the company's fiscal 1982 report would be impressive even for a firm with a happier financial history: five years of steadily increasing sales, and earnings topping $207 million. "For the first time since 1967," the report's opening statement tells us, "Lockheed's independent accountants' opinion was issued without qualification."

In all ways, the 1982 Lockheed report is a celebration of that newly recovered strength. Designed by Carl Seltzer of Cross Associates' Newport Beach, California, office, its visual format bears some of the classic elegance that has become the hallmark of that firm, while its text and editorial direction are straightforward and strong.

"Our goal was to show the corporation's strength and skill and the scale and diversity of its operations," comments Seltzer. As for his own input, he adds, "We used a simple, strongly organized design, fine type, and wonderful 4-by-5 photography."

Like most Cross-designed reports, this one was set in metal type, using what Seltzer calls "a beautiful classic face," Aldus. Contiguous hairline and four-point rules key operations text and caption blocks, respectively; in the financial section, these rules are used separately to delineate topics and totals.

But, the striking photography notwithstanding, it is the selective use of papers and printing that creates much of

LOCKHEED CORPORATION   1982   ANNUAL REPORT

the report's richness. A warm-gray laid text, used for operations copy, has been interleaved with a sturdy gloss sheet whose bright white surface frames each of ten jewel-like photographs. The soft surface of the text sheet, printed with black and earthy tones of red, green and brown, heightens the drama and sparkle of the full-color images.

Interestingly, the designer also chose to print black-and-white portraits of the chairman and the president on the gray text sheet, alongside the letter to shareholders. This decision caused some difficulties in reproduction, and the portraits had to be scanned and proofed several times before he was satisfied.

However, Seltzer's greatest personal satisfaction came from the opportunity to design the Lockheed report again after a hiatus of about five years (he had designed several of them while employed with another firm). Since that time, Lockheed management has changed. Says Seltzer, "It was real nice of them to want me to do it, and it's by far *my* best Lockheed report."

Report: Lockheed Corporation 1982. Aerospace research and craft, shipbuilding. 1982 sales $5.6 billion.
Design firm: Cross Associates, Newport Beach, CA
Art director: James Cross
Designer: Carl Seltzer
Photographer: Ken Whitmore
Copywriter: Ron Meder
Printer: Anderson Litho
Size: 8½″ by 11″; 50 pages plus covers
Quantity: 92,000

The gleam of metal and a thoughtful mix of papers create a strong report for a once-troubled aerospace company.

67/Annual Reports

Lomas & Nettleton Financial Corp.

Lomas & Nettleton Financial Corporation (LNFC) is a company whose annual reports are consistently thoughtful, literate, and well-designed. Over the years, several have appeared in various Casebooks, and the one shown here follows the LNFC tradition.

In its 1982 annual report, LNFC sought to make a special point about the changes that have occurred in the housing market in recent years, and to describe how those changes have affected young people now entering that market for the first time.

"Rather than recite a lot of statistics," says Stephen Miller, the Richards, Sullivan, Brock associate who designed the report, "we tried to make the problem more personal by interviewing a number of graduating college seniors. They discussed their chance of ever owning a home. In most cases, the outlook was not very hopeful."

To emphasize the gravity of the problem, the designers developed a modified yearbook format for the theme/photo pages. Following LNFC style, these alternate with a running text that serves as both letter to shareholders and operations review.

The yearbook look begins on the report's cover, where a black-and-white photo the size of a snapshot depicts a university's graduation exercises. The shot is simply labelled, "The Class of '82." Inside the front cover, 20 black-and-white head shots of college-aged men and women are grouped, yearbook style, against a black background. Opposite, on the opening page of the report proper, a poignant

Annual Reports/68

text asks us to recall the year we graduated from college, and all of the hopes and aspirations we felt then. Among them, the copy suggests, was the great American dream—that of owning one's own home— "one that has faded for this year's graduating class, possibly for many classes, for many years to come."

Inside, the report continues in the same visual and verbal mode. On each photo spread, a yearbook-style photo that shows one of the interviewees with some of his or her classmates sits at the top of the left-hand page; below and to the right is a brief identifying text, followed by a quote from the individual. Opposite is a full-color bleed portrait of each graduate. The portraits are somber and brooding, placing each figure against a background which, whether building or landscape, seems to dwarf the subject. In contrast to the carefree "yearbook" snaps opposite, they indicate a feeling of concern.

Locating the students for these portraits proved more difficult than the designer had anticipated. Although only six graduates were used, many more than that had to be interviewed to guarantee the proper range of backgrounds (geographic locations, majors, colleges, etc.) among students whose stories were truly interesting.

The photo pages also carry two devices which link them visually with the financial section. The first is the use of fine blue rules, which run behind large initial caps at the beginning of each caption block; they appear later as the ground for bar graphs. The other

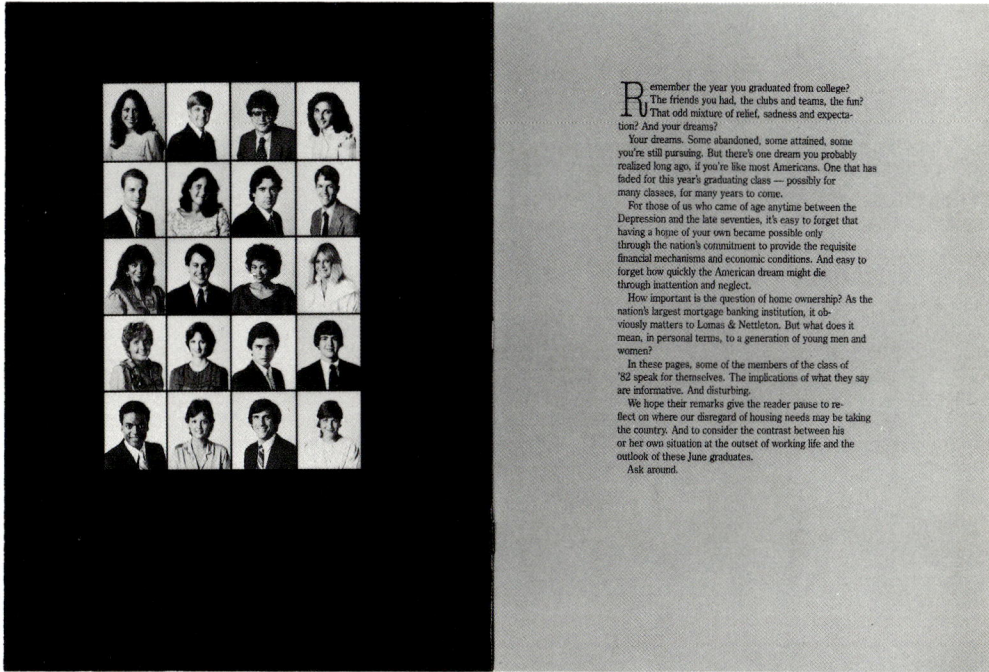

69/Annual Reports

device is actually a color: run as a band below the "yearbook" photos, this khaki-like hue forms a backdrop for a one-line tag in the theme section and reappears in the back of the book as one of the colors used in the charts.

The nation's housing problems are made more personal in this report for a mortgage investor through interviews with young people who have yet to purchase their own homes.

Report: Lomas & Nettleton Financial Corporation 1982. Mortgage banking and short-term real estate banking. 1982 revenues $134 million.
Design firm: Richards, Sullivan, Brock & Associates, Dallas
Art director/designer: Stephen Miller
Photographer: Greg Booth
Copywriter: John Stone/RSB; Jess Hay/LNFC
Printer: Heritage Press
Size: 8½" by 11"; 52 pages plus covers
Quantity: 22,500

Annual Reports/70

Pennsylvania Hospital

The Katz Wheeler design firm in Philadelphia has produced five annual reports for the Pennsylvania Hospital, a community-oriented health-care facility affiliated with the University of Pennsylvania. For each of these, the client has developed a different theme of relevance to the community which it serves.

Sometimes, the theme is more broadly defined, as in the hospital's 230th report (fiscal 1981; the reports are marked by succession, rather than by year) where it focussed on energy, conservation, and the economy; the year before that was more proscribed, and highlighted food preparation. But the reports have at times also taken unusual forms—one was a television script dramatizing rising health-care costs and their effect on low-income Americans.

The 231st annual report (1982) was both specifically focussed and unusual in form. Its first objective was to highlight the hospital's "Feeling Fit" program, a flexible health promotion campaign it markets to corporations, community groups, and individuals. But the client also wanted the form of the report to be unusual enough for recipients to read and save it. And, because budget considerations were also important, the report had to be such that it could be modified for use as a "Feeling Fit" promotional piece for several years.

Pennsylvania Hospital's public relations director, Dolores Ziff, with whom the designers worked on the project, suggested a poster/calendar promotion piece with a separate, bound annual report

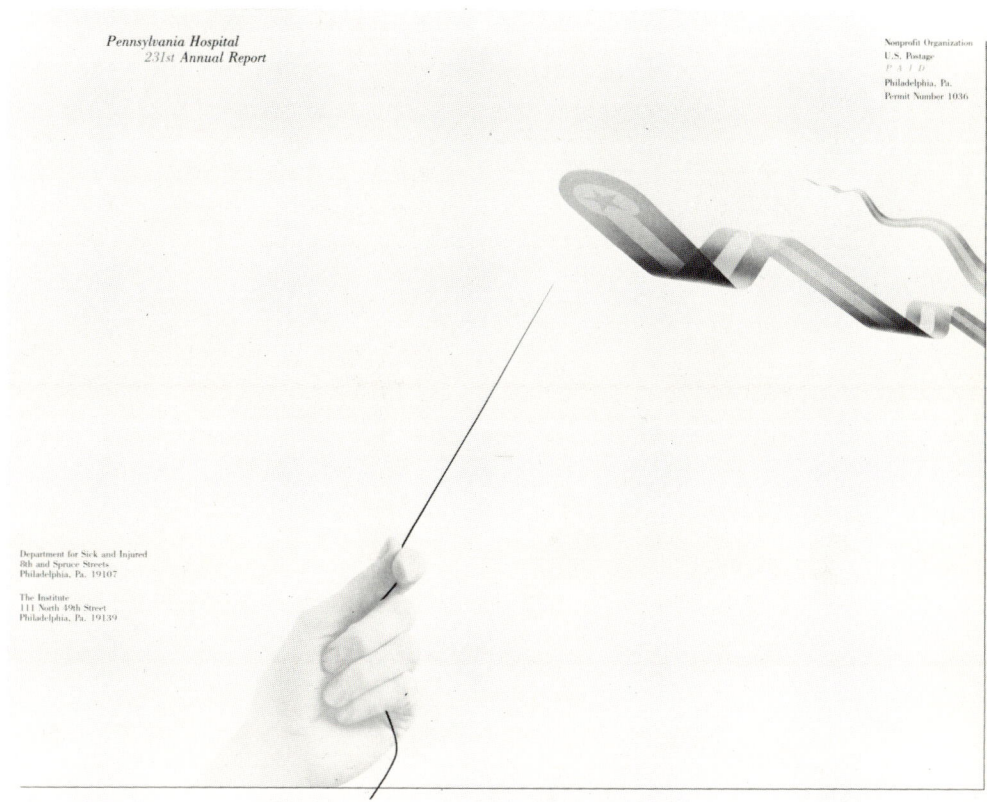

71/Annual Reports

to be mailed together in a tube. But after studying the problem, art director Alina Wheeler and designer Charles Menasion came up with another idea.

"We conceived of integrating the two functions in a single piece," says Wheeler, "under the title line '52 Alternatives to Jogging,' which provided the structure for the design. On one side we planned a poster/calendar with information that was timeless, and on the other, information that was annual-report specific. The title set a tone for health being fun and suggested an upbeat treatment."

Following the demands of the problem, Wheeler designed the piece with a split personality. Beginning with the envelope, which boldly initiates the design of the poster and functions as a cover, she paid particular attention to the way in which the reader would enter into the report. As he or she progresses from the poster's folded, 8″ by 12¾″ size, the recipient reads the president's message (illustrated with a large-dot, silhouetted photo of a diver in the midst of a jack-knife) and then, opening further, finds various listings concerning hospital officers, board, and affiliations.

At this point, the poster is nearly fully opened; only two vertical folds remain. Opening the first reveals the hard data—revenues, funds, and balance sheet—and offers the first peek at the "fun" part of the solution inside. The reader has now seen all of the report proper, except for tables showing hospital auxiliary and patient statistics, which information has been tucked on the "back," that is, on the blind panel shared with the poster "cover" page and the high diver.

This annual-report part of the solution has been printed in black and medium blue on one side of the poster sheet; its format utilizes each of the nine "blocks" formed by the folded poster as a separate horizontal page. Each page is laid out to a four-column grid, of which the extreme left is white space.

The poster/calendar side of the sheet continues this format on a large, single-unit scale. The poster's full 38¼″ width boasts 12 columns of "52 Alternatives" text, with a 1983 calendar running in a strip across the bottom.

If the reverse side of the poster was designed for business, this one is pure pleasure. Set into and under the text are a variety of images, some illustrations and some photographs, some useful to the text and some not. Comprised of 52 numbered bits of advice, the text itself is not an exercise plan but a compilation of ways to lead a healthier, less stressful life. Some of the suggestions are predictable—quitting smoking, for example, or eating less. But others are simple and sensible ideas that if we do think of, we don't take seriously enough—

taking time to ourselves each day, eating the right foods, communicating candidly with those around us. Still others are specific tension-relieving or get-up-and-go tricks, pointed plugs for the hospital's fitness program, or quotes from philosophers on improving the quality of our individual lives.

Production for this side of the poster demanded some tricks in itself. Wheeler wanted to use two colors, with one being a split fountain. This demanded an overall design that would be forgiving of that method's unpredictability on press. It also demanded a printer capable of the process, which Wheeler discovered is now considered an outdated mode of production. Finally, the bright colors specified called for a bright white, 70-pound sheet with high opacity—in this case, Poseidon text.

The finished piece met all of the designers' and the client's demands and has even exceeded some of their expectations. "People have called from all around the country requesting copies," Wheeler reports; "they appear to be reading and responding to the information. Corporations have been buying them in quantity to hang on their walls—it's a modest investment for a health message. And, in terms of the client's pattern of annual reports, this report has to be one of the most unusual. It was a challenge to our ingenuity, and the client regards it as a total success."

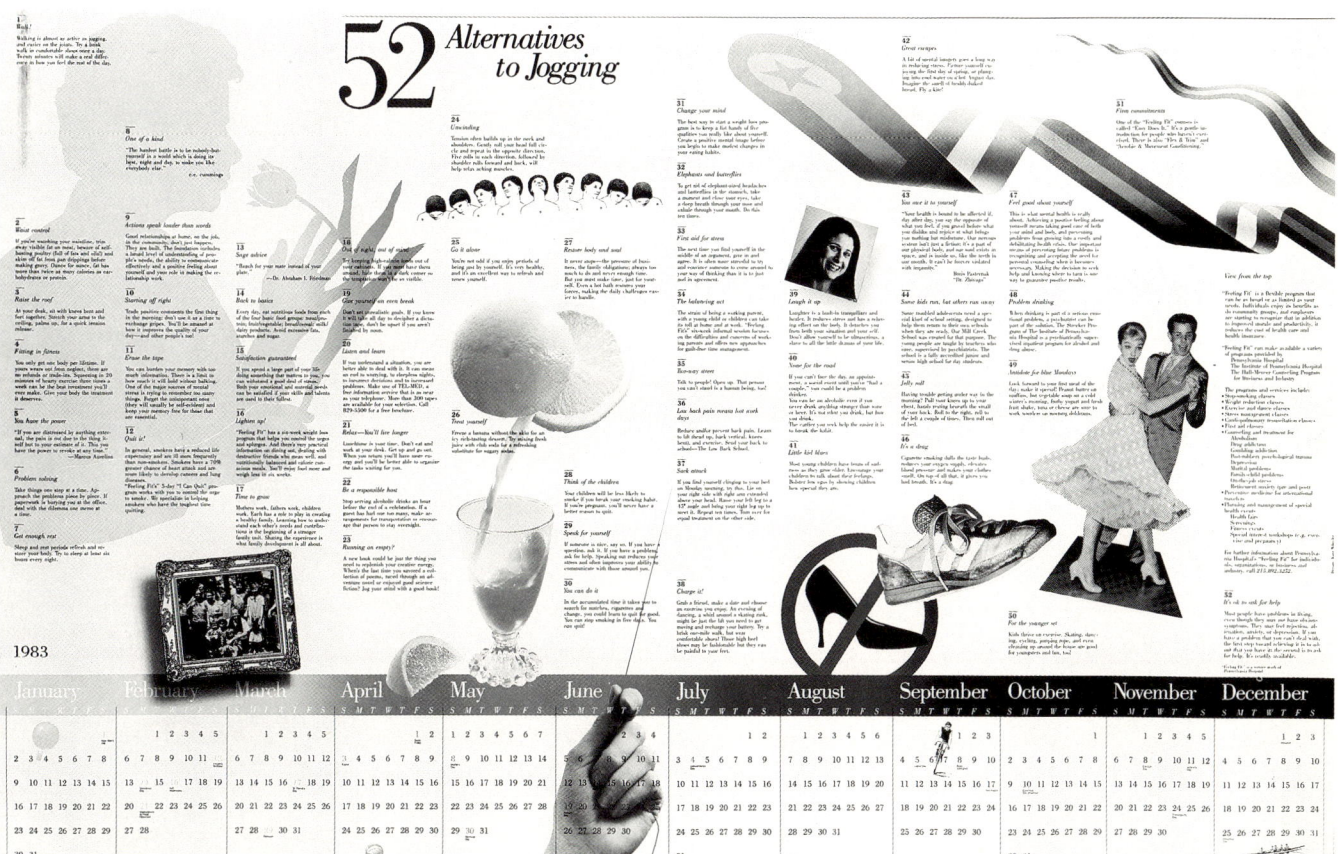

An unusual and highly keepable poster/report for a hospital gives healthy advice all through the year.

Report: Pennsylvania Hospital 231st (1982). Community health care. 1982 revenues $113 million.
Design firm: Katz Wheeler Design, Philadelphia
Art director: Alina R. Wheeler
Designer: Charles Menasion
Photographer: Deborah Pannell
Illustrator: Stacey Lewis
Copywriter: Dolores Ziff/Pennsylvania Hospital
Size: 8″ by 12¾″ (folded); 24″ by 38¼″ (unfolded)
Quantity: 10,000 as annual reports; 3,000 as posters

73/Annual Reports

Amerada Hess

In the previous Annual Reports Casebook, another Amerada Hess annual report presented a strong case for the company's management in a period of difficulty for the petroleum business worldwide. That report, dated 1979, was a glossy and colorful production.

The 1981 Amerada Hess report is one of a different color—or, more accurately, no color. Its serious, conservatively black-and-white execution reflects the changes that have occurred in the oil business and their effects on companies which, like Hess, have made considerable investment overseas.

This report has no theme statement, no explicit subtext to its operations review. Rather, the news is presented, straightforwardly, in the letter to shareholders: In 1981, a worldwide surplus of both crude oil and refined petroleum products, a serious recession in the industrialized nations, energy conservation practices that reduced demand for oil, and the use of alternate fuels in response to high oil prices all conspired to cause a drop in the price of products. Yet oil-producing countries refused to lower their prices on crude. Thus, Amerada Hess and others suffered heavy losses on purchase contracts. Although its revenues for the year were a modest $1.5 million over those of the previous year, earnings per share dropped from $6.44 to $2.53.

The operations review follows the letter without fanfare. Its visual format is the same: wide columns of text set one to a page in a readable Cheltenham face, with hairline and three-point rules setting off

small-cap headlines and tabular material.

This simple solution receives strong support from a simply captioned photo essay which begins on the cover and winds through the first half of the report. Shot in square format, the high-contrast black-and-white photos picture a range of Amerada Hess operations, from oil-drilling operations in the fields of North Dakota to refineries in the Virgin Islands to a self-service gas station near Reading, Pennsylvania. It is probably no accident that the company's holdings in places like Libya and Abu Dhabi are not represented: these are trouble spots, and the photos used reflect the company's emphasis on more secure explorations and installations, such as those in the U.S. and its territories and among our allies in the North Sea.

The financial section is designed with similar restraint: tables and notes using the same rules and typefaces, printed in a two-column format on a stippled glove-gray sheet.

This report is the first produced for Hess by Corporate Graphics, and its art director, Bennett Robinson, tells us that he wanted to report the company's operations "in a businesslike and low-keyed" mode. Not only has he succeeded in that objective; he has also managed to maintain the strong corporate image created by other designers in earlier—and flashier—reports.

JACK-UP RIG BEING SET IN PLACE IN THE GULF OF MEXICO

GAS PLANT IN NEW ULM TEXAS

The serious state of oil affairs is aptly reflected in this conservative, black-and-white report for an oil producer.

Report: Amerada Hess 1981. Oil and gas production, refining, and marketing. 1982 total revenues $9.4 billion.
Design firm: Corporate Graphics, New York City
Art director: Bennett Robinson
Designer: Paula Zographos
Photographer: Kim Steele
Copywriter: Terry Garcia
Printer: Sanders Printing
Size: 9" by 11"; 52 pages plus covers
Quantity: 100,000

75/Annual Reports

Times Mirror

The Times Mirror Company is perhaps best known as the owner of the Los Angeles Times, but this publishing giant has other interests as well. In addition to its five metropolitan and three community newspapers and over a half-dozen book imprints, Times Mirror operates seven broadcast television stations and cable television systems in 16 states, publishes several popular magazines, owns newsprint operations and a commercial printing company, and produces assorted art and graphics products.

Despite the declining economic environment of recent years and the demise or consolidation of some of the nation's better-known newspapers, Times Mirror has continued expanding operations within its areas of expertise—and posting record results.

The two Times Mirror reports elected to this Casebook reflect the company's attitude of strength. Both were designed by the Robert Miles Runyan office in Los Angeles, and, while each has its own esthetic and its own focus, there is remarkable consistency in their design and execution.

In the 1981 report, this strength is represented through diversity: an assortment of images, most of which originally appeared in Times Mirror publications during 1981. A few of these are editorial cartoons, but most are photographs—or more precisely, photojournalism.

And they are as varied as events covered by Times Mirror publications: R. Buckminster Fuller seen through and above one of his geodesic domes; Los Angeles

Dodgers pitcher Fernando Valenzuela headed for the dugout; New York City's Mayor Ed Koch marching in a parade. But not all of the subjects are so well-known; there are also some youngsters practicing soccer with their school team and unidentified firefighters battling a blaze. And when the pictures aren't from Times Mirror publications, they are special photos made to illustrate a particular facet of the company's business—its television stations, for example, or the timberlands that feed its newsprint operations.

Because these images are both black-and-white and color as well as of diverse shapes and sizes, this report relies heavily on its design to create a feeling of cohesiveness. Throughout, photos are positioned at the top of the square page and float in the generous white space created by confining the running text to the lower third. Deviations from this norm are few, with an occasional image allotted a page of its own. Some of these loners are bordered by a thin white rule and completely surrounded in black, much like the image on the report's cover. (There seems to be no particular reason for this deviation, other than to offer contrast to the uniformity of the other pages and because, after all, these pictures do look good that way.)

In fact, designer Jim Berté has used black as a unifying element throughout the operations review. It appears here and there as a background color, and each of the photographs has been hung from a broad black rule that abuts its upper edge. A subtle touch, but an effective one.

77/Annual Reports

Two reports for a West Coast publisher: one draws images from Times-Mirror publications . . .

In counterpoint, short (two-pica) rules of the same weight, printed in an earthy brown, have been dropped into the text to mark the beginning of each discussion in the business-by-business reportage. These brief bars reappear in the financial pages, completing the visual transference from black to brown and again creating unity in diversity. In this latter section, their color further serves to enhance the warmth created by a beige text sheet.

By contrast, Times Mirror's 1982 report had a more cohesive look from the outset. Here, according to Berté, "the objective was to use well-known persons endorsing Times Mirror products." All of the photographs were made by one man, photographer Bruce Davidson, and his singular vision combines with a more strictly structured format to create a tight little report.

In this book, white is the watchword. Normal report proportions have returned, but the layout is horizontal, serving up a crisp white Kromekote-and-Quintessence surface on which to place Davidson's square, full-color portraits.

Typographic and graphic elements are kept simple: Text is set in four columns of Aldus ("because it sets 'small'"); the top of each page is edged with a hairline rule. On text pages, a demi-bold headline sits atop the rule; on photo pages, identifying tags sit both above and below. The esthetic is carried through into the financials, where the format is two-column and the paper is a warm white, stippled text.

With text and page layout so understated, these brilliant photographs are real eye-

Times Mirror

1982

Annual Report

. . . the other features well-known personalities who read these publications.

79/Annual Reports

Newspaper Publishing

Although Times Mirror's newspapers performed relatively well in 1982 despite a weak economy, the American newspaper industry as a whole experienced a difficult year. While newspaper circulation reached all-time highs — more than 61 million on weekdays and more than 55 million on Sundays — there were isolated instances of newspaper closures and evening publications folding into morning editions.

Revenues for the Newspaper Publishing group in 1982 reached $1.14 billion, a 7% increase over the previous year, but operating profit decreased 12% to $149.7 million. This decline in operating profit is primarily attributable to lower classified advertising linage at most of the Company's newspapers and to the cost of programs designed to improve competitive positions in the Dallas and Denver markets. Both *Newsday*, on Long Island, and *The Hartford Courant*, in Connecticut, recorded very strong performances despite the soft economy.

In 1982, the Newspaper Publishing group consisted of eight daily newspapers: the *Los Angeles Times*; *Newsday*, on Long Island; the *Dallas Times Herald*; *The Denver Post*; *The Hartford Courant*; *The Advocate* and the *Greenwich Time*, both in Connecticut; and the *Orange Coast Daily Pilot* in Southern California. The Orange Coast Publishing Company, which publishes the *Daily Pilot*, was sold to a company affiliated with Ingersoll Publications in February 1983.

The management of each Times Mirror newspaper recognizes that newspapers must be innovative in content, in format, and in circulation strategy in order to survive recessionary times and the increasing competition for readers' time. These factors were evident at all of the Company's newspapers during 1982.

To strengthen editorial coverage, numerous news bureaus were opened throughout the country. *The Times* relocated its Southern bureau from Atlanta, Georgia, to Miami, Florida, a move that both enhances domestic coverage and provides more accessibility to coverage of events in the Caribbean. The *Times Herald* opened Toronto, New York, and Middle East–Cairo bureaus.

New editorial sections covering such topics as business, food, fashion, entertainment, home decorating, and local news were introduced at many of the newspapers. In addition, *The Hartford Courant* premiered a new Sunday magazine, titled "Northeast," and the *Dallas Times Herald* introduced a Mid-Cities section designed for readers residing in the area between Dallas and Fort Worth. At *The Denver Post*, weekly zoned editions were restyled and increased from five to eight advertising zones.

Topping the list of more than 40 first-place awards given to the *Los Angeles Times* was the Pulitzer Prize for music criticism presented to Martin Bernheimer, the newspaper's classical music critic. In addition, the Society of Professional Journalists, Sigma Delta Chi, presented its distinguished public service award to *The Times* for its coverage of regional crime patterns and, for the second consecutive year, gave its award for editorial cartooning to Paul Conrad. A Pulitzer Prize was also awarded to Art Buchwald of the Los Angeles Times Syndicate.

E. Cardon Walker Chairman Walt Disney Productions

Los Angeles Times

"*The Times*' comprehensive coverage of the world, and most particularly of the entertainment and business communities, has made it essential reading at Walt Disney Productions for many years."

Other Operations

The Other Operations group contains two distinct lines of business: magazine publishing and art and graphic products.

Revenues for the group were $189.4 million, an increase of 7% over the 1981 figure. Operating profit rose 4% to $17.2 million primarily due to a strong performance in magazine publishing.

More magazines are being published now than ever before. Through the past decade, the number of Audit Bureau of Circulation member magazines rose 39% to a total of 419. Circulation per issue for ABC publications rose 18% during the same period.

Advertising revenues at Times Mirror Magazines, Inc. rose nearly 15% in 1982, three times the rate of growth for the industry as a whole. Two newsstand sales leaders, *Popular Science* (circulation 1.8 million) and *Outdoor Life* (circulation 1.5 million), are among the 50 circulation leaders in the country. The number of advertising pages at *Popular Science* in 1982 increased 7% over the 1981 figures, while revenues increased 14%.

Outdoor Life posted a 1% decline in ad pages over the same period but finished the year with a 7% increase in revenues.

Seven consecutive issues of *Ski Magazine* (circulation 421,000) broke every advertising page and revenue record of its 47-year history.

Golf Magazine (circulation 774,000) increased newsstand sales. The magazine also publishes *TOUR* and *FAIRWAY*, the official publications of the Professional Golfer's Association and the Ladies Professional Golfer's Association.

Times Mirror Magazines also operates the *Outdoor Life* and *Popular Science* book clubs, which together sold more than 5.5 million books in 1982.

The Sporting News Publishing Company, located in St. Louis, Missouri, publishes *The Sporting News* and *The Sporting Goods DEALER*, a publication for the sporting goods trade.

The Sporting News circulation of more than 506,000 reflects readers' acceptance of the magazine's 1981 format changes and improved graphics. Compared to 1981, the year of the baseball players' strike, the number of advertising pages in *The Sporting News* increased a dramatic 20% in 1982.

The company also publishes a number of annual football, basketball, and baseball record books, as well as *The Sporting Goods Directory*.

The art and graphic products group consists of Chartpak, Plan Hold Corporation, and M. Grumbacher, Inc.

Results at Plan Hold, a manufacturer of architectural and engineering equipment, and at Grumbacher, the leading art materials company in North America, fell below expectations due to a recession-related slowdown in consumer spending.

Conversely, Chartpak, manufacturer of graphic and drafting supplies benefited from a strong performance as a result of product line extensions, such as new type faces and template designs, which augmented its full range of transfer lettering, charting tape, film, signage, symbols, and engineering supplies. Adding to Chartpak's success was its entry into industrial product production, and penetration of the office products market.

Grumbacher also introduced several new product lines in 1982, among them synthetic Bristolette brushes and the Designer line of sable brushes. New products introduced in the last three years now account for almost 20% of sales.

In a move to increase the number of active painters, Grumbacher began testing its step-by-step painting instruction classes on television and has achieved encouraging results. Six hour-long programs are now cablecast in Detroit and five programs are broadcast on the Public Broadcasting station in Tampa, Florida.

In 1982, Plan Hold introduced a new graphic arts chair, a wire roll for desk-side or mobile rolled storage, and a modular system for filing, storing or mailing log films and prints.

Whitey Herzog General Manager and Manager St. Louis Cardinals, 1982 World Champions

The Sporting News

"Winners tend to seek out other winners. They have a style, a look, a respect you can sense. The Cardinals have it. So does *The Sporting News*."

---

catchers. And the quality of Davidson's eye—his sensitivity to lighting and form, his feel for color and composition, and the minimal distortion of his lens—creates a kind of other-worldly character in many of these shots. There is a group of nurses clustered around a Times Mirror textbook in a hospital ward, their faces lifted deadpan to the camera. There's the director of the Oregon Department of Environmental Quality, also photographed from above, with mounds of baled wastepaper looming up behind him. There's a world-class diving champion standing before his luminescent pool, his rippling red muscles reflecting the rosy glow of a setting-sun sky.

The mood here is confrontational (though not hostile); as the subjects peer into the lens, we sense their seriousness, their credibility, and their need to know. By their appearance in this report, we understand and trust the commitment of the Times Mirror company to match that credibility and to meet their needs.

Annual Reports/80

Report: Times Mirror Company 1981 and 1982. Newspaper and magazine publishing; newsprint and forest operations; book publishing; information services; broadcast and cable television; art and graphic products. 1981 revenues $2.15 billion; 1982 revenues $2.21 billion.
Design firm: Robert Miles Runyan & Associates, Los Angeles
Art director: Robert Miles Runyan
Designer: Jim Berté
Photographers: Various (1981); Bruce Davidson (1982)
Copywriter: Times Mirror
Printer: George Rice & Sons
Size: 9½" by 9½"; 56 pages plus covers (1981); 11" by 8½"; 48 pages plus covers (1982)
Quantity: 60,000 (1981); 65,000 (1982)

81/Annual Reports

Peat Marwick

Peat Marwick International Annual Review 1982

Peat Marwick International (PMI) is a privately held accounting partnership and, as such, is not required by law to issue an annual financial statement. Hence, the 1982 Peat Marwick "annual review" has no section devoted to financial tables and notes. Still, it does perform many of the functions of the contemporary annual report. It describes the nature and scope of PMI's business, and its use of annual report devices—such as discrete sections for a chairman's letter and a review of operations—puts it, from a design standpoint, squarely in the league of more strictly defined annual reports.

But the PMI 1982 report was also to be used extensively for promotion and sales development, and Pentagram designers Peter Harrison and Susan Hochbaum worked with PMI's director of publications, Gerry Barry, and art director Chris Rubin to develop a concept that would satisfy both reporting and promotional goals. The result is a document set apart from those produced by other big accounting firms.

The report is divided into three parts—the two already mentioned, plus a photo section presenting case histories of various PMI clients. And it is this last section that comprises the major thrust of the book. Here, photographs by Neal Slavin show various PMI partners "on the scene" with both large and small clients, or present those clients alone. These are not conventional shots of executives in action, however, but more symbolic photographs which lend both drama and elegance to the report. One shot, for example,

Annual Reports/82

was taken in the mirrored showroom of a leading Paris couturier; the true focus of the picture—a display of perfume produced by PMI's client, Revlon—is merely incidental to the feeling conveyed. A few spreads later, client Colin Davies, whose company designs and produces computer-oriented forms, stands among his former co-workers at the British coal mine where he got his start.

But if these photographs provide drama, it is the review's design that provides its overall cohesiveness. "We wanted to do something with allusions to the layout of an accounting book," says Harrison, "with ruled pages. But we also wanted to impart a certain dignity—a sort of semi-classical grace."

His "accounting book" feeling was effected with ultra-fine gray rules running between lines of text. (In the front of the book, this text sits in two ragged columns; in the photo section, it sits in one column whose lines are centered.) Double rules along the top, right, and left spread margins separate headlines and folios while furthering the ledger "look"; the addition of marbleized vellum end papers and a tall and narrow page format seal it.

Although, due to budget restrictions, the designers were forced to drop one matched color, the overall design didn't suffer. And, while headlines were changed from a script face to the Bodoni Antiqua used for the text, the copy retains a traditional elegance. One paper—Vintage Gloss in text and cover weights—was used throughout.

83/Annual Reports

Photos in this annual "review," run full-color and double-truck, portray PMI partners and clients around the world.

Report: Peat Marwick International 1982. Accounting partnership. 1982 fees earned $1.15 billion.
Design firm: Pentagram, New York City
Art director: Peter Harrison
Designer: Susan Hochbaum
Photographer: Neal Slavin
Copywriter: Gerry Barry/PMI
Printer: Sanders Printing
Size: 8¼" by 11¾"; 24 pages plus covers
Quantity: 45,000

Annual Reports/84

Eli Lilly

How near to perfection can an annual report be?

The Eli Lilly Company 1981 annual report, the first designed for this client by Corporate Graphics in New York, was deemed near enough that it was one of only two reports to be elected unanimously to this Casebook.

Indeed, this is a report with tremendous appeal, with warm photographs of Lilly users by Bruce Davidson and full-color illustrations by Wilson McLean spotting the operations review. And while the report makes use of other, more conventional annual report "parts," it is the excellence of their overall orchestration which makes the whole greater than their sum.

Like other reports reviewed in this Casebook, this one downplays the operations review in favor of a special theme. Printed against a warm gray background that is approximated by a text sheet used later in the report, the look of the operations text is strengthened by large initial caps and bold black rules running at the bottoms of the pages. The paintings, which in McLean's super-realist style serve as somewhat symbolic interpretations of Lilly's several businesses, are both complex and compelling and, had they been reproduced at a larger scale, could have served well as the major visual interest of the report. It is only their size and artful dropping into the text that minimize their impact.

Although there is little in Lilly's operations story to require a shift of emphasis (both sales and earnings were up in respectable amounts), it is the following photo section that delivers the real message of

this report and positions Lilly, according to the opening theme statement, as one of several firms "who create products that improve the satisfaction of basic human needs." Some of these products, the copy continues, save lives, relieve pain, restore health, or enhance appearance; others increase food supplies in a hungry world.

The photo section seeks to further humanize Lilly's businesses by presenting the faces and stories of nine individuals whose lives were improved by Lilly products. There is an infant whose life was saved by a Lilly antibiotic; an older woman, shown hanging draperies in her home, thanks Lilly for restoring the use of her arthritic hands. Chatting with students, a university instructor leads a relatively normal life because of a Lilly insulin pump, and a Japanese rice farmer stands smiling in a paddy that is protected from disease with a Lilly fungicide.

The photos are large—they fill seven columns of each eight-column spread—and imposing and quite captivating. In some cases, the distortion caused by the camera lens serves to heighten the intensity of the portrait by lending a documentary-like immediacy; in others, the camera falls back, as if to let the scene create itself. "The photography is this report's biggest draw," says its art director/designer, Bennett Robinson. "People really live in those pages, and working with Bruce Davidson to get those shots was one of the best parts of the job."

"Most of all," he adds, "we strove for total believability," and it would seem as though this objective were achieved.

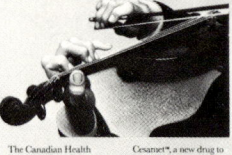
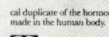
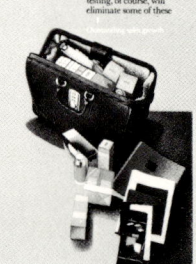

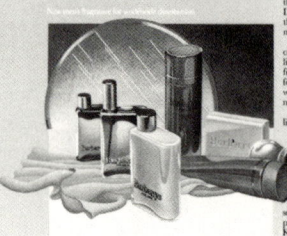

With their moody, incidental lighting and gentle, glossy finish, their naturally styled presentation of "real people," and their brief but convincing case histories alongside, these photographs go a long way to making Lilly appear a company who cares.

A pharmaceutical report with a double dose of appeal: an illustrated operations section, and a special photo essay revealing how Lilly products improve the quality of human lives.

Report: Eli Lilly and Company 1981. Medicines and medical instruments, agricultural products, cosmetics. 1981 sales $2.8 billion.
Design firm: Corporate Graphics, New York City
Art director: Bennett Robinson
Designers: Bennett Robinson, Paula Zographos
Photographer: Bruce Davidson
Illustrator: Wilson McLean
Copywriter: Tom Ritman
Printer: The Hennegan Co.
Size: 9" by 11"; 58 pages plus covers
Quantity: 107,000

87/Annual Reports

SCM

For SCM Corporation, 1981 was a year of mixed results. Although sales were up slightly and totalled $1.94 billion at the company's June 30 year-end, operating income dropped eight per cent; similarly, while dividend per share increased, its well-known typewriter and appliances business operated at a loss.

Despite this unevenness, SCM took steps in 1981 to position itself as a strong, innovative corporation with an eye to producing results in the long term. First, the company invested over $34 million in research and development, an area of spending which for the past five years SCM has been steadily increasing. Then, SCM introduced the Typetronic, its first electronic typewriter and an important product of this research. And finally, the company initiated its first corporate advertising campaign, utilizing full-page ads in the Wall Street Journal to tell readers that SCM believes in the importance of R&D.

The SCM 1981 annual report was conceived to bolster this message. Like several reports appearing in this Casebook, it makes use of a vertical organizational structure which includes a special section for a special purpose. The operations review in this book—a mere six pages of gem-like product still-lifes and brief operational reports—has been significantly reduced to make room for a photo essay that delivers the real message of the report: innovation.

This message is first boldly heralded with a one-word, vertical headline at the opening of the 11-page photo essay. "It's important to remember that

'innovation' isn't limited to glamorous items like computers, lasers and genetic engineering. An innovation is anything new or improved, whether esoteric or mundane," says the over-sized position statement that follows and fills the first page of the section. "Innovation is time-consuming and expensive," the copy later continues, "but it is a necessary process if SCM is to remain a leader in the five basic businesses in which we are involved."

What follows are bold and bright photographs of those businesses. Reproduced on a large scale and accompanied by smaller, more explanatory photographs or diagrams, these photos work to involve the reader with some recent SCM advances.

"We used a slightly bigger page size," comments art director Arnold Saks, "to establish as large a format as possible. We wanted maximum impact, as well as more space for copy." The copy blocks accompanying the photos are set flush-left in the Caledonia reader and semi-bold weights used throughout the book; they are linked visually to operations and financial reports by consistent use of Scotch rules to head new topics or pages.

Saks reports that the only difficulty in producing the report—his first for SCM— was met by over-seeing color reproduction. "We solved it," he reports, "by using a terrific printer, excellent color separations, and excellent printing on Heidelberg presses."

As one Casebook juror summed up this report: "It presents as informative and

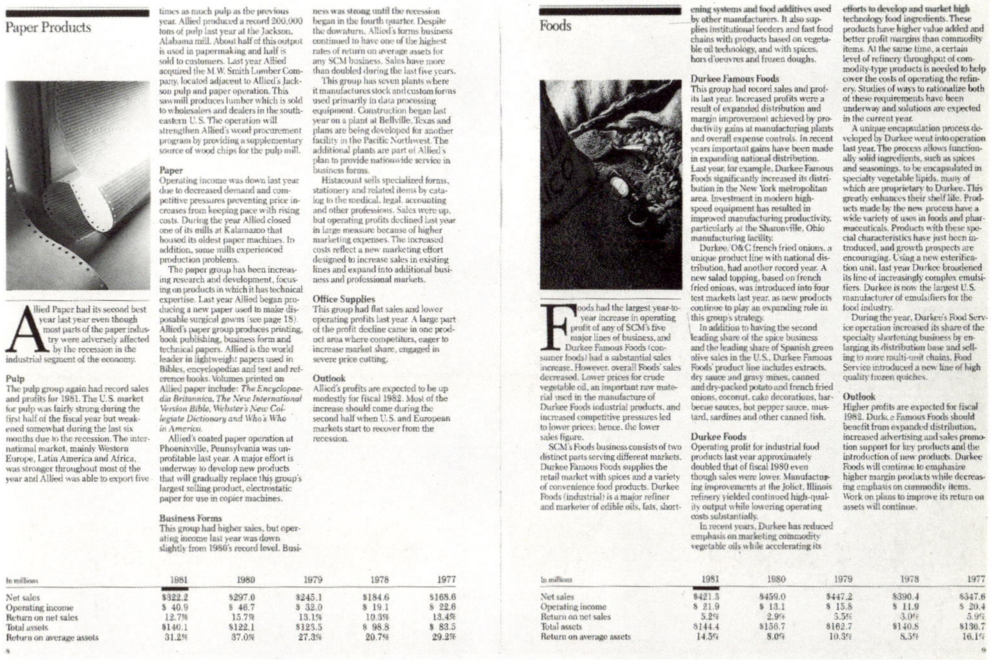

Paper Products

Allied Paper had its second best year last year even though most parts of the paper industry were adversely affected by the recession in the industrial segment of the economy.

Pulp
The pulp group again had record sales and profits for 1981. The U.S. market for pulp was fairly strong during the first half of the fiscal year but weakened somewhat during the last six months due to the recession. The international market, mainly Western Europe, Latin America and Africa, was stronger throughout most of the year and Allied was able to export five times as much pulp as the previous year. Allied produced a record 200,000 tons of pulp last year at the Jackson, Alabama mill. About half of this output is used in papermaking and half is sold to customers. Last year Allied acquired the M.W. Smith Lumber Company, located adjacent to Allied's Jackson pulp and paper operation. This company produces lumber which is sold to wholesalers and dealers in the southeastern U.S. The operation will strengthen Allied's wood procurement program by providing a supplementary source of wood chips for the pulp mill.

Paper
Operating income was down last year due to decreased demand and competitive pressures preventing price increases from keeping pace with rising costs. During the year Allied closed one of its mills at Kalamazoo that housed its oldest paper machines. In addition, some mills experienced production problems.

The paper group has been increasing research and development, focusing on products in which it has technical expertise. Last year Allied began producing a new paper used to make disposable surgical gowns (see page 18). Allied's paper group produces printing, book publishing, business form and technical papers. Allied is the world leader in lightweight papers used in Bibles, encyclopedias and text and reference books. Volumes printed on Allied paper include: *The Encyclopaedia Britannica*, *The New International Version Bible*, *Webster's New Collegiate Dictionary* and *Who's Who in America*.

Allied's coated paper operation at Phoenixville, Pennsylvania was unprofitable last year. A major effort is underway to develop new products that will gradually replace his group's largest selling product, electrostatic paper for use in copier machines.

Business Forms
This group had higher sales, but operating income last year was down slightly from 1980's record level. Business was strong until the recession began in the fourth quarter. Despite the downturn, Allied's forms business continued to have one of the highest rates of return on average assets for any SCM business. Sales have more than doubled during the last five years.

This group has seven plants where it manufactures stock and custom forms used primarily in data processing equipment. Construction began last year on a plant at Bellville, Texas and plans are being developed for another facility in the Pacific Northwest. The additional plants are part of Allied's plan to provide nationwide service in business forms.

Histacount sells specialized forms, stationery and related items by catalog to the medical, legal, accounting and other professions. Sales were up, but operating profits declined last year in large measure because of higher marketing expenses. The increased costs reflect a new marketing effort designed to increase sales in existing lines and expand into additional business and professional markets.

Office Supplies
This group had flat sales and lower operating profits last year. A large part of the profit decline came in one product area where competitors, eager to increase market share, engaged in severe price cutting.

Outlook
Allied's profits are expected to be up modestly for fiscal 1982. Most of the increase should come during the second half when U.S. and European markets start to recover from the recession.

In millions	1981	1980	1979	1978	1977
Net sales	$322.2	$297.0	$245.1	$184.6	$165.6
Operating income	$ 40.9	$ 46.7	$ 33.0	$ 19.1	$ 22.6
Return on net sales	12.7%	15.7%	13.1%	10.3%	13.4%
Total assets	$140.1	$122.1	$125.5	$ 98.8	$ 83.5
Return on average assets	31.2%	37.0%	27.3%	20.7%	29.2%

Foods

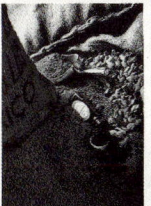

Foods had the largest year-to-year increase in operating profit of any of SCM's five major lines of business, and Durkee Famous Foods (consumer foods) had a substantial sales increase. However, overall Foods' sales decreased. Lower prices for crude vegetable oil, an important raw material used in the manufacture of Durkee Foods industrial products, and increased competitive pressures led to lower prices; hence, the lower sales figure.

SCM's Foods business consists of two distinct parts serving different markets. Durkee Famous Foods supplies the retail market with spices and a variety of convenience food products. Durkee Foods (industrial) is a major refiner and marketer of edible oils, fats, shortening systems and food additives used by other manufacturers. It also supplies institutional feeders and fast food chains with products based on vegetable oil technology, and with spices, hors d'oeuvres and frozen doughs.

Durkee Famous Foods
This group had record sales and profits last year. Increased profits were a result of expanded distribution and margin improvement achieved by productivity gains at manufacturing plants and overall expense controls. In recent years important gains have been made in expanding national distribution. Last year, for example, Durkee Famous Foods significantly increased its distribution in the New York metropolitan area. Investment in modern high-speed equipment has resulted in improved manufacturing productivity, particularly at the Sharonville, Ohio manufacturing facility.

Durkee O&C french fried onions, a unique product line with national distribution, had another record year. A new salad topping, based on french fried onions, was introduced into four test markets last year as new products continue to play an expanding role in this group's strategy.

In addition to having the second leading share of the spice business and the leading share of Spanish green olive sales in the U.S., Durkee Famous Foods' product line includes extracts, dry sauce and gravy mixes, canned and dry-packed potato and french fried onions, coconut, cake decorations, barbecue sauces, hot pepper sauce, mustard, sardines and other canned fish.

Durkee Foods
Operating profit for industrial food products last year approximately doubled that of fiscal 1980 even though sales were lower. Manufacturing improvements at the Joliet, Illinois refinery yielded continued high-quality output while lowering operating costs substantially.

In recent years, Durkee has reduced emphasis on marketing commodity vegetable oils while accelerating its efforts to develop and market high technology food ingredients. These products have higher value added and better profit margins than commodity items. At the same time, a certain level of refinery throughput of commodity-type products is needed to help cover the costs of operating the refinery. Studies of ways to rationalize both of these requirements have been underway and solutions are expected in the current year.

A unique encapsulation process developed by Durkee went into operation last year. The process allows functionally solid ingredients, such as spices and seasonings, to be encapsulated in specialty vegetable lipids, many of which are proprietary to Durkee. This greatly enhances their shelf life. Products made by the new process have a wide variety of uses in foods and pharmaceuticals. Products with these special characteristics have just been introduced, and growth prospects are encouraging. Using a new esterification unit, last year Durkee broadened its line of increasingly complex emulsifiers. Durkee is now the largest U.S. manufacturer of emulsifiers for the food industry.

During the year, Durkee's Food Service operation increased its share of the specialty shortening business by enlarging its distribution base and selling to more multi-unit chains. Food Service introduced a new line of high quality frozen quiches.

Outlook
Higher profits are expected for fiscal 1982. Durkee Famous Foods should benefit from expanded distribution, increased advertising and sales promotion support for key products and the introduction of new products. Durkee Foods will continue to emphasize higher margin products while decreasing emphasis on commodity items. Work on plans to improve its return on assets will continue.

In millions	1981	1980	1979	1978	1977
Net sales	$421.3	$459.0	$447.2	$390.4	$347.6
Operating income	$ 21.9	$ 13.1	$ 15.8	$ 11.9	$ 20.4
Return on net sales	5.2%	2.9%	3.5%	3.0%	5.9%
Total assets	$144.4	$156.7	$162.7	$140.8	$136.7
Return on average assets	14.5%	8.0%	10.3%	8.5%	16.1%

Innovation

The pictorial essay on the following pages is about innovation at SCM. We think this is a subject of deep significance for all American industry, not just SCM's small part of it.

It's important to remember that "innovation" isn't limited to glamorous items like computers, lasers and genetic engineering. An innovation is anything new or improved, whether esoteric or mundane. We consider the innovative process so important to SCM's future that it was selected as the theme of our first corporate advertising program, launched earlier this year. Using full-page advertisements in *The Wall Street Journal*, we tell readers that through research and development the people of SCM are constantly working to invent new products and improve existing ones.

Innovation is time-consuming and expensive, but it is a necessary process if SCM is to remain a leader in the five basic businesses in which we are involved. New products and processes are developed to meet a variety of business objectives. Some recent SCM innovations: an electronic office typewriter that sells for less than most electric office models, a water-based liner for beer and beverage cans that meets environmental standards while saving energy, a new, energy-efficient toaster, an improved liquid shortening that enables bakeries to be more efficient. Most important, each of these products has already made or is soon expected to make an important contribution to SCM profits.

On a larger scale, innovation is vital in all industries if America is to remain at the forefront of technology and maintain its position in world markets that in recent years has been eroded by foreign competition.

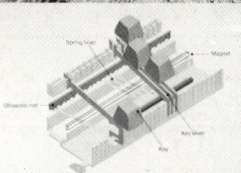

The Brain Behind Typetronic
The integrated circuit (above) is the "brain" that controls Smith-Corona's Typetronic™ electronic office typewriter. The 30,000 transistors on the circuit contain logic that enables them to perform many tasks, among them remembering the last ten characters typed, so that they can be corrected automatically. The "brain" also evaluates data from the ultrasonic red (left) to determine which key has been struck. All 30,000 transistors are on a silicon chip less than one-quarter inch square.

89/Annual Reports

clear a story as any book on the table." "The table" held all of this Casebook's winning reports.

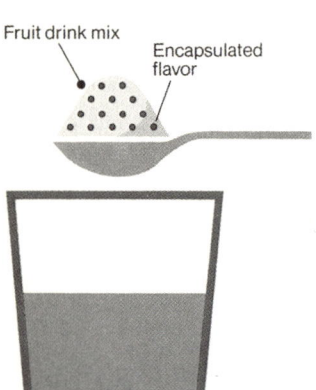

Bold and brightly colored photographs of various SCM research and development projects visualize the theme of this report—innovation.

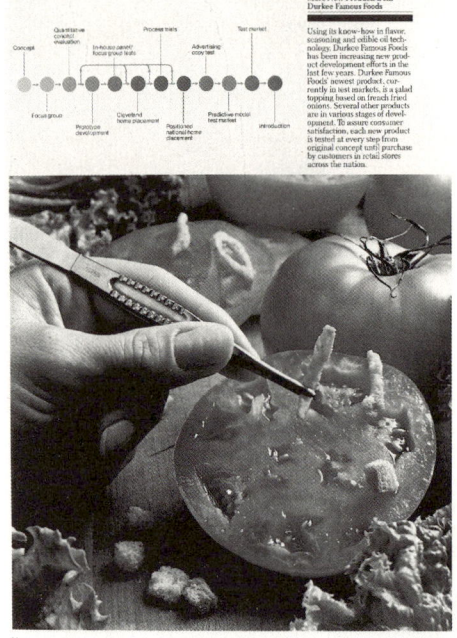

Report: SCM Corporation 1981. Chemicals, coatings, and resins, paper products, foods, typewriters and appliances, industrial processing equipment. 1981 net sales $1.94 billion.
Design firm: Arnold Saks, Inc., New York City
Art director: Arnold Saks
Designer: Robert Jakob
Photographer: Gary Gladstone (cover and reportage), Peggy Barnett (product photography)
Copywriter: Herb Katz/SCM
Printer: Case-Hoyt
Size: 9" by 11½"; 44 pages plus covers
Quantity: 135,000

Annual Reports/90

Convergent Technologies

What does a company do with its first annual report?

Convergent Technologies, the premier supplier of desktop workstations to original computer equipment manufacturers, was founded in August 1979. Through the third quarter of 1980, Convergent remained in a research and development phase, and first production units were shipped by the end of that year. By the end of 1981, the company's first full year of production, revenues from sales topped $10 million. In 1982, Convergent went public—and its revenues were in excess of $96 million at year end.

When Lawrence Bender was asked to design Convergent's 1982 annual report—its first—he wanted "to find a quiet and conservative way to scream about a terrific company." And if his means of achieving that goal by presenting a who-we-are, what-we-do, where-we're-going picture of the company sounds mundane, the execution of that concept definitely wasn't.

"Because of rapid sales/earnings and stock price growth, the client wanted to project a conservative image," comments Bender, who art-directed the report. "Thus we used black-and-white photography instead of color. The photos, extremely dark, with Rembrandt-style lighting, were fitting for a private company newly public—its debut."

A kind of touchstone for the book is the image which appears on its cover—a paper napkin on which has been scribbled, with arrows, underlines, and asterisks, the original strategy for the

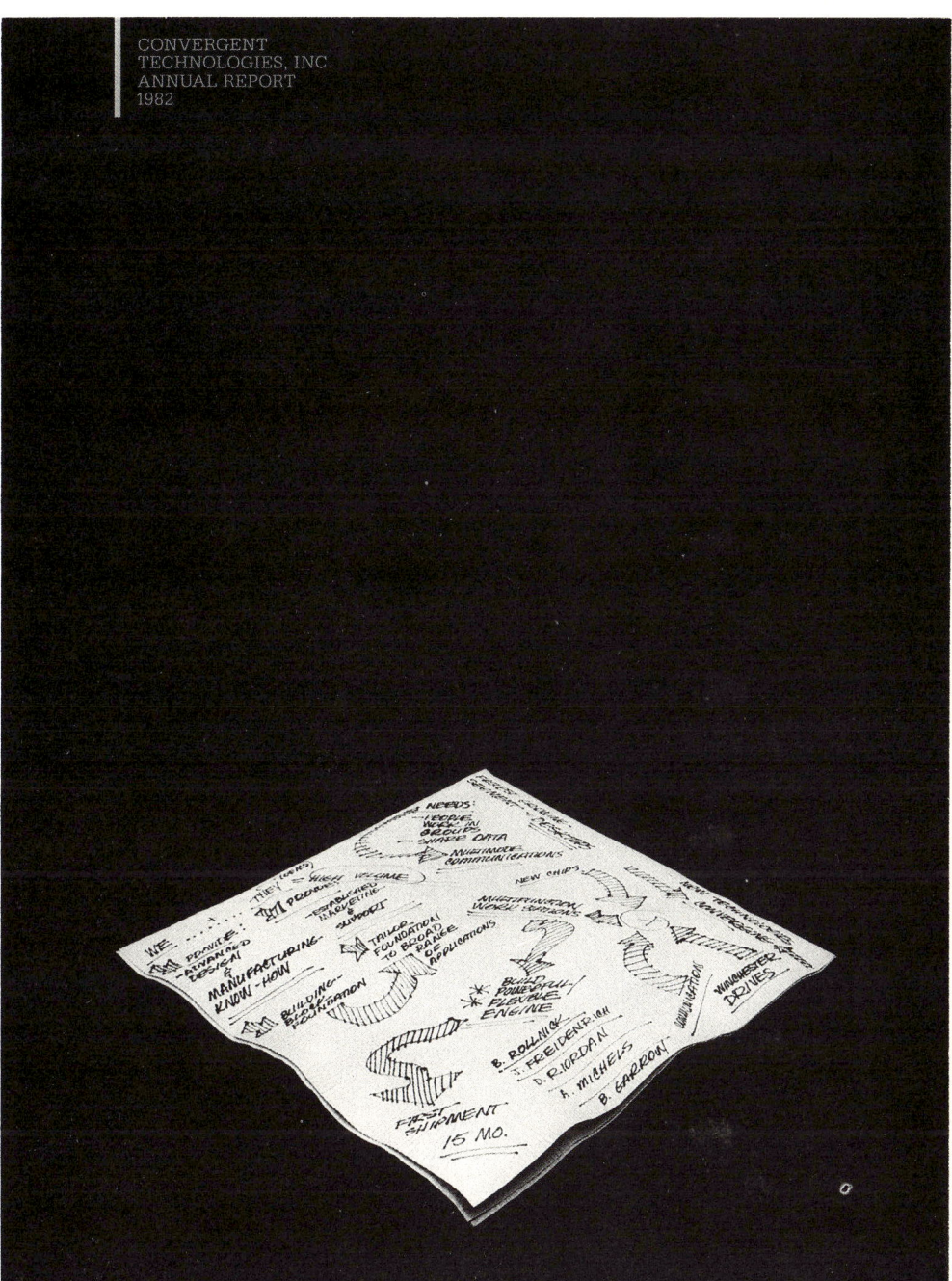

founding of the firm. Sitting in the spotlight at the bottom of the cover, the napkin is eye-catching by its presentation and serious by its content. In this one image, Bender has already succeeded in screaming with conservatism.

That image is brought home on the next spread, where financial highlights are presented at the top of a darkened page. Below, still in the spotlight, the napkin has been opened to reveal the sales projections from that early business plan. A simple comparison shows that, in 1982, Convergent had already doubled what it had hoped to be earning by 1984. The message is powerful: the casual idea, scrawled during a business lunch, parlayed into a multi-million-dollar company.

This style of immediacy continues through the report. The carefully lit photos of people-and-computers are run bleed across the slightly oversized spreads, and, while Tom Tracy's pictures are strong and serious enough in themselves, the designers have added some subtle but stunning effects: text is run in a narrow column or columns and printed in the gray used in the scanned tri-tone photographs; a single short but hefty rule protrudes into each photo from top and bottom trim lines. Printed in the clear cadmium yellow that lines the report's covers, the rules point up headlines and offer bright counterpoint to the pages' velvety, matte-varnished blackness.

Bender had only two-and-a-half months to produce this report; he showed Convergent's president, Allen Michels, and Sandy McCardell of investor

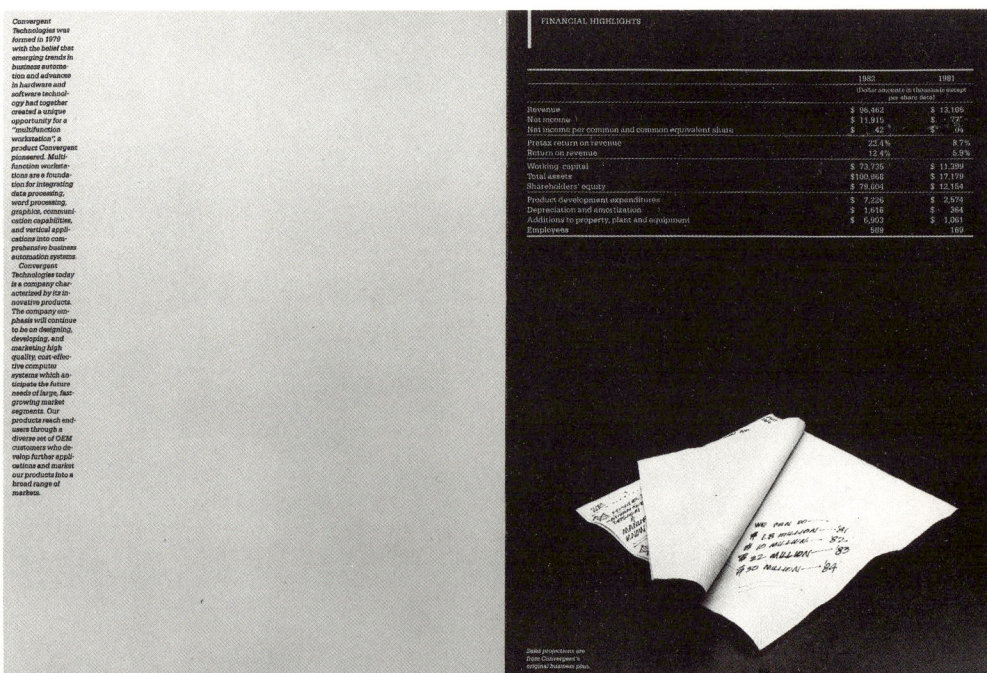

relations only a thumbnail representation—not his usual way of working. "The client trusted us to go directly to finished art," says Bender, "and of course approved the report at the art/mechanical stage."

For his client's very first annual report, a designer finds "a quiet way to scream about a terrific company."

Report: Convergent Technologies, Inc. 1982. Computer system design and development. 1982 sales $96.5 million.
Design firm: Lawrence Bender & Associates, Palo Alto, CA
Art director: Lawrence Bender
Designer: Linda Brandon
Photographer: Tom Tracy
Copywriter: Convergent Technologies
Printer: Anderson Litho
Size: 8¾" by 11¼"; 28 pages plus covers
Quantity: 30,000

Marline Oil

In fiscal 1982 the Marline Oil Corporation made some changes in its business.

When Marline became an active natural-resource operating company in 1976, the larger part of its assets consisted of Canadian gas reserves. In November 1981, owing to recent Canadian regulations placing financial and operating constraints on businesses owned by non-Canadians, Marline sold these assets.

Secondly, and more significantly, Marline announced in July 1982 that it had discovered an important uranium deposit in the State of Virginia. And, finally, the following month, Marline purchased Poolquip, a holding company which wholesales swimming pool supplies and equipment, to generate cash flows for the company's explorations programs.

While all of this business had to be revealed in Marline's 1982 annual report, it was the second point that shaped the book's visual presentation. Marline had begun an intensive uranium exploration program in 1977, at first on a continental scale and later, based on initial findings, focussing on a specific formation in south-central Virginia. With the pay-off announced in 1982, it was implicit that Marline's design firm, Gluth, Weaver of Houston, develop a report which would address various aspects of the proposed uranium development program.

One of these areas was, as Al Gluth describes it, "presenting a favorable outlook on uranium exploration." Because vast quantities of ore are required to produce a

relatively small amount of the mineral (Marline's find, which is expected to yield four pounds of the precious stuff per ton of ore, is considered "higher grade"), and because of various environmental concerns associated with uranium mining itself, Marline wished to reassure its audience that it is fully aware of its environmental responsibilities. And, while this point is addressed head-on in the textual review of Marline's minerals exploration operations, it is more subtly and perhaps more effectively conveyed in the accompanying photographs.

Environmental views often carry emotional associations, and, as in past Marline reports, designer Gluth has made positive use of this phenomenon. For this one, he selected moody pictures made by Arthur Meyerson of the Virginia countryside, and their compelling nature suggests that the photographer's sensitivity to the environment is part and parcel with Marline's.

The mood established in the minerals section through scenes of rolling hills covered with fall foliage, or a small community nestled into a twilighted countryside, is extended to the second part of Marline's operations review—a discussion of its oil and gas drilling business, which is conducted primarily in the onshore Gulf Coast areas of Louisiana, Mississippi, and Texas. Here, the full-page color photos reveal a mist-shrouded Texas landscape or a gas drilling rig silhouetted against a darkening sky. The fact that all of the report's pictures were made at sunset or with what appears to be the warm, thin light of late afternoon is an

95/Annual Reports

Oil & Gas Drilling Operations

Beginning in fiscal 1979, the Company has organized and managed four annual drilling funds, which have undertaken drilling operations primarily in the onshore Gulf Coast areas of Louisiana, Mississippi and Texas.

additional unifying element.

Gluth has opened each of the two sections with double-page color photos of workmen taken from overhead. The brightly colored hard hats, the tools of the trade, the almost vulnerable appearance of the flesh-and-blood workers against the backdrop of a cold steel floor, have an immense appeal. We find that in looking over their shoulders and seeing what they are doing, we are curious to know more about them—and about Marline.

Each of these larger photos, like the smaller, full-page ones illustrating the operations reviews, are bordered in black. A soft gray band, with dropped-out type, identifies the section; below it an italicized copy block, also dropped out of a dark section of the photo, encapsulates the highlights of the copy to follow. The black and gray motif adds both drama and a sense of the serious and is echoed by the large black initial caps and gray bars that relieve the widely set operations text.

This report also makes use of a production variation seen more and more in smaller annual reports: the double saddle wire. While bigger, perfect-bound reports have long been able to mix and shuffle papers with ease, only recently has technology allowed saddle-stitched books to do the same. The Marline report uses two colors of Quintessence Gloss, ivory and white, wrapping the former around the latter so that opening statements and contents page are printed on the same sheet as the financial review.

Crisp industrial and moody landscape photography reflect the dual concerns of this energy company: running a profitable business without damage to the environment.

Report: Marline Oil Corporation 1982. Oil, gas, and minerals exploration and development; swimming pool supplies. 1982 revenues $26.8 million.
Design firm: Gluth, Weaver, Inc., Houston
Art director/designer: Al Gluth
Photographer: Arthur Meyerson
Copywriter: Marline
Printer: Grover Printing
Size: 8½" by 11"; 40 pages plus covers
Quantity: 8,000

Annual Reports/96